TEMPORARY MOM

A Foster Parent's Journey Through Love and Loss and the Lessons God Taught Me Along the Way

BESS LEWIS

© 2018 Bess Lewis

All rights reserved. No part of these publications may be reproduced, distributed, or transmitted in any form or by any means, including photocopying, recording, or other electronic or mechanical methods, without the prior written permission of the publisher, except in the case of brief quotations embodied in critical reviews and certain other noncommercial uses permitted by copyright law.

For permission requests or inquiries, please contact: tbcflewis@gmail.com

Printed in the United States of America

Unless otherwise noted, Scripture quotations taken from:

The Holy Bible, New International Version (NIV). Copyright 1973, 1978, 1984 International Bible Society. Used by Permission. All rights reserved.

All rights reserved.

ISBN-13: 978-1717287526
ISBN-10: 1717287522

ACKNOWLEDGMENTS

With sincere gratitude:
To Jeanette Windle – my editor
To my Mom Carol Evaul, Uncle Phil Evaul, Mother-in-Law Debbie Lewis, Grandma Janet Kern and Dear Friend Angie Gorman for proofing my book and for all the loving advice along the way.
To Philip Eppard "Pancho" for designing the cover of the book.
To everyone who contributed their experience with the foster care system and allowed me to publish it here in this book.
To my birth kids: Caleb, Faith and Lydia for enduring a busy mom while she documented this journey.
To my best friend, Tim – being my greatest encourager as we walk together obeying our Creator and preparing here on Earth for a glorious eternal future together celebrating Jesus.
To Jesus - who makes all things possible and is the Source of all love and goodness.
May this book show many the way to him…

DEDICATION

I dedicate this book to all 'temporary moms' – the work is hard with little appreciation but it is the best job in the entire world with rewards that can change the course of history eternally.

Table of Contents

PROLOGUE 1

1 THE CRY OF A MISSIONARY HEART 5

2 SEEING THE NEED 13

3 PERSISTENCE 23

4 THE CALL 33

5 THE WAKE-UP CALL 43

6 VISITS 57

7 DISCIPLINE 71

8 REACTIVE ATTACHMENT DISORDER 85

9 SEEKING SOLUTIONS 95

10 UNSEEN BATTLE 107

11 THE DARKEST MOMENT 119

12 THE LONG WAY "HOME" 129

13 LOSS AND GRIEF 141

14 A DIFFERENT POINT OF VIEW 151

15 JOURNEY TO A MIRACLE 157

16 OUR MIRACLE 165

17 FULL CIRCLE 177

APPENDIX ONE: 189

A TRIBUTE TO THE CHILDREN WE LOST AND LOVE 189

APPENDIX TWO: 195

PRAYERS FOR THOSE WHO FOSTER 195

PROLOGUE

> *The placement decision must be made more expeditiously because growing up cannot be put on hold, and the impact of being without a permanent family is felt each day by a child.*
> —Washington State Supreme Court Justice Bobbe J. Bridge

As I packed tubs of toys and clothing, I reminded myself that my husband and I had been called and prepared to do what had been set before us. God had predestined our particular family for this very moment. But grief overwhelmed my heart, and my mind could not get past its pain to comprehend God's plan in all this. In fact, all I could see at this moment was loss.

I glanced over at the two darling children who had been part of our family for almost three years. Their expressions as they looked back at me were bewildered and frightened at what today's events meant for their future. Coughing back my tears, I forced a smile.

"Everything's going to be okay," I managed to say, but it was myself I was trying to reassure.

Six-year-old Kay-Kay accepted my reassurance and began playing with some toys waiting to be placed in a tub. But her eight-year-old brother T-Man burst out frantically, "Mommy, I don't want to go! This is my home! You are my family!"

At his plea, my tears welled up, my heart bursting. I reprimanded myself sternly: *"Be strong, Bess! Be an adult. Be mature."*

What I was really telling myself was to be emotionless, to be fake. But if I melted and showed my heart, wouldn't that just make the inevitable even more painful for T-Man? Again, I pushed down my tears and cleared my throat.

"Honey, this is how God wants it. I don't understand it, but God wants all of us to obey. He gave you a daddy who wants you back. In fact, he *needs* you back. And if God is sending you away, then God promises to go with you. If Jesus thinks you can do this, then so do I. I don't want you to go, and I love you. But God wants you to go and be with your daddy. We both need to trust Jesus that he knows what is best. Do you think we can do that together?"

T-Man turned his head away, mumbling some answer under his breath. I gave him a hug and continued packing up the two children's possessions. Tomorrow he would be gone. Tomorrow she would no longer call me Mommy. Tomorrow my heart would split in two. Tomorrow would be a day full of broken dreams and shattered desires.

God, give me the strength to face tomorrow! I pleaded silently.

You see, tomorrow my role as their foster mother would be over. Not that I ever thought of myself as a *foster* mother to these children. I had fallen completely in love with them. In my heart, I was their mother. The word "foster" for me meant temporary, short-term, interim. I wanted to belong to these children forever, permanently, securely.

When you believe something is not forever, you end up loving just half-way. So I'd given these children my all, my best. I'd withheld no love from them. I'd poured out my heart, accepted that which wasn't birthed to me. For a truly good foster parent must also be a broken parent. Because when you love, you break. You give away forever a part of your heart. Christian theologian and philosopher C. S. Lewis says it best:

> "To love at all is to be vulnerable. Love anything, and your heart will certainly be wrung and possibly be broken. If you want to make sure of keeping it intact, you must give your heart to no

one, not even to an animal. Wrap it carefully round with hobbies and little luxuries; avoid no entanglements; lock it up safe in a casket or coffin of your selfishness. But in the casket—safe, dark, motionless, airless—it will change. It will not be broken; it will become unbreakable, impenetrable, irredeemable . . . The only place outside Heaven where you can be perfectly safe from all the dangers . . . of love . . . is Hell."
— (The Four Loves)

To love is not bliss. The journey of loving is a crooked, winding, difficult mountain of patience and pain. Love requires great courage and endurance that can only come from a Source stronger and more powerful than itself. Because I have been shown great love and because this Love lives in me, then I am compelled to *give* love. The very act of loving is sacrificial as the actual words of Jesus remind us:

> "The greatest love you can show is to give your life for your friends." (John 15:13, GW)

I did not so easily surrender my desire to make these two children part of our forever family. The journey I will share with you in the following pages is a story of my personal struggle with the foster care system. But it is also a story of my own naivety and sin of self-righteousness that led me to believe I was the better parent. I believed these children were better off in my care and their birth parents deserved to lose their kids. After all, a parent who abuses and neglects their own flesh and blood should never get a second chance, right?

Let me share with you the nitty-gritty of my personal walk of purification in loving. And how through it my thoughts became transformed as God used pain and loss to teach me about my own great need of second chances.

1 THE CRY OF A MISSIONARY HEART

The call of missions is to love Jesus in such a way that you don't need a specific event or place to witness, but that from a heart desiring to see humanity saved, we live every single moment committed to being witnesses of the Gospel and its transforming power.—Anthony Jermaine

My heart has always been set on missions. I can credit my parents for this gift. My parents became missionaries to the South American country of Bolivia when I was just four years old. My dad was himself a missionary kid (MK), born in Colombia and raised as well in Chile and Ecuador, all South American countries.

In total contrast, my mother was born and raised in the same small town of Millersville, Maryland, near the Chesapeake Bay. When she married my father, who was then working in a secular career as a salesman, she had never traveled overseas. Still, it was her spirit and drive that inspired my father to use his MK know-how in returning to the mission field. They'd been married ten years by then and had three daughters, of whom I was the middle one (a fourth child, our brother Bobby, would be born overseas). At her encouragement, my parents packed up their fair-skinned, blue-eyed children to head to an extremely foreign and poverty-stricken new home, specifically the country of Bolivia in central South America.

There my parents were assigned to oversee a mission base outside Bolivia's lowland city of Santa Cruz as well as to work with special needs children. Later they were assigned to manage a training center for Bolivian pastors, that had its own farm with pigs, goats, cows, and horses, so I grew up knowing both city and country life. Unlike my father, Mom knew not a word of Spanish, but with fearless determination, she hired herself a tutor, practiced on everyone she met, and was soon fluent.

My mom wasn't just fearless, but from my earliest childhood, she imprinted on my soul the joy of giving. She didn't just give when it cost her nothing, but when it hurt. When it was an inconvenience. Like the rainy day we were driving into Santa Cruz for school in our double-cab, four-wheel-drive pickup when she noticed a man shivering in the cold on the side of the road. Stopping the vehicle, she jumped out, peeled off her own jacket, and wrapped it around the stranger.

Or there were the many times my mother stopped to offer a ride to some pedestrian walking along Bolivia's dusty, unpaved roads. Which meant that we children had to give up our own seats inside the cab and retire to the truck bed where dust coated our faces and our teeth gritted with sand. But we also learned to appreciate and have compassion on those less privileged, giving them our place so that they might possibly see Christ through us.

It was my mother's daily example that taught me to have a spirit of courage and a heart of compassion for lost, hurting souls. Her fiery-red hair was a depiction of the fire God had placed inside her soul for his people. She always noticed the lowliest servants who were part of our missionary life: the maids, farm boy, gardener, the lady who washed our clothes by hand. And in noticing them, she also gave them a place in our home so that somehow a farm boy hired to milk our goats would end up sitting at our family table to eat with us. For her, nothing was too farfetched or impossible for God.

My father was the stability of our family, his predictability a comfort to my soul. He was deeply grounded in God's Word, and I can remember constantly debating with him about the Scriptures. He never saw any question as senseless or immature but encouraged his children to open the Bible so we could find answers together.

My father was also incredibly adaptable. Having been a missionary kid himself, he understood two cultures and the battle that exists inside an MK's soul to belong to both and neither at the same time. My father forced me out of my comfort zone to speak to people I didn't want to speak to, whether that meant having compassion on some homeless street kid who was yanking at my hair to get a sample of my blonde tresses or translating for visiting Americans who all seemed to us kids so wealthy, clean-smelling, and impeccably dressed.

Dad taught me to stand tall and be strong. If there is one inheritance I received from him, it was his desire to see lost souls come to Christ. I can remember traveling with him to the Bolivian countryside to show the Jesus film. He would set up a generator and movie projector in some village where they had no electricity. After showing the movie, Dad would share God's plan of salvation with the villagers. I would be in the front row, pleading with God to touch hearts and lead many to repentance.

Both of my parents included all four of us children in their ministry. They exposed us to the realities of hurting people and did not safeguard us from experiencing the culture of the people they served. I attended a Bolivian school for junior high and high school, the only blonde-haired, blue-eyed student in my class. While my skin tone might not have matched my classmates, my heart moved to a Latin rhythm. I'd never known any life outside of missions, and I had full confidence I would live out my own life in some Spanish-speaking country, helping its neediest citizens and following our family legacy by becoming a third-generation missionary.

In truth, I don't know who I would be today if I didn't have such a great family. My parents not only led me to faith in Jesus Christ, but they effectively modeled to me Christ-like love. I felt compelled to share this gift that my parents had given me. The gift of knowing what a loving, Christ-like family is.

My husband Tim's upbringing was starkly different from mine, but just as clearly marked by a strong Christian heritage. Tim was the firstborn son of a fifth-generation farming family from a small town in southern Illinois. Corn, soybeans, and wheat provided their income. From Tim's birth, his mother prayed that her first-born son would have a tender heart and be responsive to God's speaking. A farmer's daughter herself, she taught my future husband to be a savvy businessman and how to manage such a high-stress job. But she also taught him to trust in God's provision, to be discerning, and to sense and obey the prompting of the Holy Spirit.

It was his mother's prayers that inspired Tim to move fifteen hundred miles from his prairie home to the rugged Rocky Mountain peaks of Montana Bible College. Encouraged by his studies there, he participated in a short-term missions trip to Thailand, where the great needs he saw deeply touched his heart. By the time he returned to his Illinois hometown, he was determined to marry someone who shared his desire to do missions.

Farming is not an easy task, and Tim's father exemplified hard work. But he also taught Tim that if you worked hard, you could play hard, always finding time to toss a ball with his son after a long, hard day or to take his family on an annual vacation. From his father Tim learned responsibility, how to manage employees, and what it meant to be a good leader. This desire to lead would encourage my husband to achieve college degrees in the field of agricultural business and go on to create his own farm business.

I was twenty-two years old when I met Tim and very set in my ways. I considered myself to be in the United States just long enough to finish a master's degree in education so I could return to the country I loved, Bolivia. I was attending Greenville University, a Christian liberal arts college in south-central Illinois. Tim's family, who lived in the town of Greenville, attended the church attached to the college, and his father led their adult Sunday school class, which is where I first met Tim.

Being a small Sunday school class, Tim noticed me immediately. He tells me I stood out like a sore thumb among other single females in the class since instead of southern Illinois's relaxed dress code of jeans and T-shirt my preferred attire was Latin-style super-high heels and somewhat shorter skirts. But when I opened my mouth, I spoke like someone who knew God's Word through and through. Intrigued, he began to pursue me.

Intimidated by his quiet, determined demeanor, I avoided Tim's invitations until one day he got the bright idea of asking if I wanted to join the church "missions team". I readily agreed. Our first missions outreach was to visit the elderly right there in our sleepy community. Tim picked me up in his brand-new, red Chevy pickup, but I soon realized no one else was joining us. He will tell you to this day that everyone else canceled, but I still have my suspicions it worked out just like he planned.

Our second "date" was just as unnerving. Tim invited me to participate in a local parade at the county fair on behalf of their family agricultural business. My role involved tossing out candy from inside a huge spray truck emblazoned with the name of their family business while he drove the truck along the parade route. The chance to do something I had never done before made me agree instantly.

When I showed up, he asked if I wanted something to eat before the parade. Making every effort to be agreeable, I responded, "Sure, I'll have whatever you are having."

That was when I learned Tim and I have very different tastes in cuisine. I had never eaten a bratwurst, and it took me a half-hour to choke it all down so he wouldn't know how much I disliked his offering. As we sat several meters off the ground inside the heavy-duty agricultural machine, Tim asked me several very direct questions. Things like whether I was willing to be a stay-at-home mom, homeschool my children, and be willing to adopt. He was bold and blunt in his queries, and even now when he retells the story, he makes clear that if I'd failed his oral exam there would be no third date.

As I considered how to respond on his adoption question, my thoughts went back to my own childhood. My home in Bolivia was close to an orphanage. Every day, a small boy from that orphanage would walk past our home and yell out to our mother, "Señora!" She would respond by sending us kids out with brownies and other American snacks.

We pleaded with our parents to adopt the boy, but to no avail. Still, his sweet smile engendered in me from that time forward an intense desire to adopt. So I could respond sincerely that I was definitely interested in adopting. I would find out in time that my answer convinced Tim I was "marrying material".

In turn, Tim quickly grew on me as he introduced me to his own culture of rural, farming America. It was a way of life I'd never experienced, and I fell in love with whatever he taught me. How to drive a semi. How to participate in a farm auction. How to celebrate an American Thanksgiving. Four-wheel-driving down dirt roads. Hunting white-tail deer. Sledding.

Tim also captivated me with his soft way of asking deep, soul-searching questions about God, missions, and life. In eight short months, he convinced me to marry him and start a life there in southern Illinois that was as foreign to me as growing up in a third-world country would be to him.

Tim assured me that our very differences would make us a powerhouse for the Lord. He brought a stability that my life of constant moves and broken relationships had never known. I brought to him the excitement of the unknown and a spirit of adventure to do something crazy for the Lord. Our wedding on November 29th, 2003, was a celebration of our combined life experiences as both country music and Latin salsa filled the church. Spanish and English were spoken throughout our marriage ceremony, and both the USA and Bolivian flags stood proudly on stage.

Our initial plans were to have no children for our first five years of marriage so we could focus on paying down bills and becoming debt-free. But just six months after our wedding day, we discovered to our complete surprise and delight that I was pregnant. The birth of our firstborn son Caleb on March 11, 2005, helped seal our marriage and banish our own natural selfish, independent natures. To be honest, our marriage had undergone some strain before my pregnancy, our two very different cultures constantly clashing. God's gift of a beautiful, healthy son who needed us impelled us to cast aside personal pride and surrender to unity instead of living for ourselves.

Sixteen months later, God again showered us with grace by giving us a daughter, Faith. Our family was complete. On the day Faith was born, Tim and I made the decision for me to have a tubal ligation so we could stay focused on our goal to adopt.

My home life was now perfect. I lived out in the lush, green southern Illinois countryside in a brand-new home Tim and I had designed. I had a garden and raised chickens. Since my husband worked for his parents, he was always close to home. Our children were the complete joy of our home. Life was pleasant.

But my missionary kid heart had not forgotten all those years I'd lived in a poverty-stricken country where there was such an immense need of homes for children. I could feel God calling me into action. I reminded my husband of our commitment to missions and adoption, but he didn't feel as I did that this was the right time. So instead I signed up to work as a translator for DCFS (Department of Children and Family Services), the state agency that deals with domestic violence and advocacy for children in abusive situations. Perhaps a few hours a week translating for Hispanics in our local area would help calm the yearning in my heart to do more for children and broken homes.

Once I started my translating job, it wasn't long before the social worker I worked with began encouraging me to get my license as a foster parent since there was a great need for Spanish-speaking foster parents. With my husband's work load, I knew he didn't have time to take the courses required to become a licensed foster parent. So every time the social worker raised the topic, I avoided giving an answer.

Unfortunately, I was also avoiding God's own prompting. But it wouldn't be long before Tim and I found ourselves staring into the faces of true, desperate need. That experience would change both of us forever.

From the Voice of Experience:

> "The best thing about fostering our little boys was how clearly God spoke to me about our situation. The fact is that he had been preparing me for this adventure most of my life. God spoke to me one frustrating day very clearly, saying, 'I have given you the desires of your heart, and now it is time for you to do this for me.'"
> —C.C. a foster and adoptive mom.

2 SEEING THE NEED

> *Safety and security don't just happen; they are the result of collective consensus and public investment. We owe our children, the most vulnerable citizens in our society, a life free of violence and fear.*—Nelson Mandela, former president of South Africa

One chilly December day in Illinois, I was asked to translate for a young Hispanic woman with two daughters, a toddler and a newborn. Her story was terrifying. She had been abused and badly beaten by her common-law "husband". He was arrested and deported back to Mexico, which then left her no way to provide for her children. To make matters worse, her landlord had served her with a two-weeks eviction notice, which would leave her homeless in the middle of the winter with two children under the age of two.

The hospital where the young woman had just delivered her baby reported her concerns and fears to DCFS. I in turn received a call to be her translator. I drove over to the address given. Her caseworker met me outside of the young mother's home. When he knocked on the door, a petite Hispanic woman opened it, then stood aside to let us in without making eye contact or saying a word.

It took several minutes of hesitation before she finally opened up and began telling her story of domestic violence. She had gruesome photos documenting the abuse and a police report she wanted translated. Her caseworker asked if she had any needs. Yes, she needed a place to stay, diapers, and clothes for her children.

As we walked back to our cars, I asked the caseworker what he would do for her. He responded, "Nothing. She's an illegal. We can't touch her. I'll call a couple churches, but I doubt they will do anything for her either."

I knew he was right in his assessment, and nothing would be done. On the drive home, I called my husband. I was astounded at his response. "Well, we have a whole empty basement here with a spare bedroom. Go pick her up."

My mind immediately started whirling with fears. This woman could be involved with a drug trafficker, for all I knew. And wouldn't taking in an illegal be conspiring to aid a criminal? My husband didn't speak Spanish, so how would he communicate with her when I had to leave the house for my own translation duties? Besides, she was single, which would make it awkward to leave her alone with my husband. No, no, no!

There were definitely more reasons to say no than yes. I decided that contacting local churches would be a better solution. Unfortunately, when I did so, they also gave more reasons to say no than yes. I decided maybe I would just buy the young mother some diapers and clothes. That should be enough. Heading to Wal-Mart, I purchased the immediate needs she'd listed. Returning to her house, I knocked on the door. She would not answer it for me, so I left the Wal-Mart bag on the front porch with a note in it and my phone number.

Whew! I'm glad that's over! I told myself. *I've done my part. Now I can go home to my own cozy life.*

But God had other plans. Before I could even reach my home, my phone was ringing. The young mother was on the other end, thankful and desperate. She told me more graphic details of her story. It was clear she wanted my help with her final need—a place to stay. With my husband's encouragement, I went to pick her and her children up.

Tim and I soon learned more of her story. Her name was Rosa, and she came from a small town in central Mexico. Her Spanish was choppy, as her primary language was a native Mexican Indian dialect. She had only a first-grade education and could not read in any language.

I also learned why Rosa would risk everything to enter the United States illegally. In Mexico, her livelihood had been picking up cow dung and selling it for fuel. She'd wanted more education, but there was never enough money. She also described lots of physical and sexual abuse she'd endured in her own home. So when a man twice her age told her of the great abundance and free food available in the United States, she abandoned everything to follow him.

Rosa told horrendous stories of their journey across the border, traveling at night, carrying jugs of water across the desert, and going thirsty when water ran out. People would drink their own urine to survive, and women were exchanged for a bottle of water. Once across the border, Rosa and her now-boyfriend made their way to Illinois where he had multiple connections. He quickly found work in a Chinese restaurant, above which they were given a single room to live.

By this point Rosa was pregnant, so she never did get a job. Since then, she had changed her name multiple times and lived in constant fear of being caught by Immigration. She also lived in fear that her ex-boyfriend, who was wanted for drug-dealing, might come back across the border.

I was spooked by her story, to say the least. I had my own two beautiful kids to protect, and we lived on a dead-end road right out in the countryside. Every night Rosa was with us, I prayed for God's protection, sometimes pacing the floor and laying my hands on the door posts of my children's bedroom.

When Rosa and her children came to live with us, I'd also expected she would pitch in to do her part with cooking and cleaning. It quickly became evident that she knew nothing of basic household chores or even the simplest Mexican recipes. She told me that back in Mexico her mother always cooked while in Illinois her boyfriend was a chef so she was not allowed to cook.

To this day, I don't know if this was just an excuse. But I was more concerned at her lack of motherly affection for her kids. She had decided not to breastfeed since government programs provided free formula. She would only feed her newborn in a car seat and would only touch the baby to change her diaper or burp her. Meanwhile, she simply ignored her older daughter until the toddler's behavior became unbearable.

I would try to explain that she needed to hold her baby or give structure to her toddler, feeling as though I was having to be mom to someone my own age. Rosa was hungry for knowledge, so I bought her a kindergarten book on the alphabet she could work on while I was away translating for DCFS. I was delighted when she quickly finished the entire book.

Calling around, I found out that Rosa qualified for a special visa given to domestic violence abuse victims. When I shared this good news, Rosa seemed distant. She accompanied me to an immigration attorney, who explained Rosa would just need to tell her story before a judge.

That night Rosa asked me to buy her a phone card. She spent hours on the phone. I know now that she was talking to her abusive ex-boyfriend, who was pressing her to join him in Mexico. The next morning Rosa informed me that all she wanted was an ID card for herself, birth certificates for her children, since they were born in the United States, and a ticket back to Mexico.

"You are going to go back to the man who abused you?" I asked her. "You know he will just do it again."

"Yes, I know," she admitted. "But that is where I belong. He is my baby's father, after all. He says he has a job and wants to take care of us."

"Fine, I will do whatever you wish," I assured her. "But my husband and I would like you to consider staying, becoming legal, and getting educated. We are willing to help you."

But Rosa's only response was a smile. So I drove her all the way to the nearest Mexican consulate three hours away in Indiana. After a five-hour wait, she emerged with an ID card identifying her as a Mexican citizen. We returned home to present her new ID at the local city clerk's office so she could get her children's birth certificates. Getting these was important, not just to prove the children were hers, but because they identified her children as American citizens. One day, her kids could return to the United States, go to college, even work here without having to sneak across the border.

I had expected some difficulty getting Rosa's paperwork, but just as at the consulate, the city clerk handed over the birth certificates without any questions. To me, this was a miracle in itself. I said to Rosa, "You know God did this!"

Rosa agreed. Her paperwork done, I asked what else she needed. She said she wanted to buy as much medicine and formula as her suitcases would fit. This broke my heart. I knew formula would be very expensive in Mexico and wondered how she would get by. If only she had made the decision to breastfeed. But we went to the store, where she used her welfare debit cards and WIC coupons to buy over twenty cans of formula. I added over-the-counter children's medicine from my own cabinets. Once Rose got to Mexico, even buying baby Tylenol would be a challenge, and I kept worrying about how she was going to make it.

Then it dawned on me. What Rosa really needed was nothing I could physically give her. She needed the Bread of Life (John 6:35), the Living Water (John 7:39)! Though we always prayed before meals and Rosa had seen me pray out loud each time we'd gone in to get her needed documents, I had not yet spoken to Rose about Jesus Christ. I knew God wanted me to present his plan of salvation to her and that I was running out of time.

I went online and ordered an audio-Bible on an MP3 player. It arrived the very next day. A full week had now gone by since Rosa had entered our home. No matter how hard we'd tried to persuade her to stay, she remained committed to leaving. Reluctantly, we agreed to drive her that evening to a Mexican *tienda*, the place of business where a charter bus heading to Mexico would be picking up passengers. This might be my last opportunity to share Jesus with her.

Saying a quick prayer, I knocked on her bedroom door. "Rosa, may I come in?"

Rosa opened the door. Her few belongings were already stacked in neat piles for packing. Sitting down on the bed beside her, I said, "It has been a joy to share our home for this short time with you and your family. But I would be no friend if I let you leave our home without sharing with you the most precious gift of all—Jesus. It is Jesus who changes lives and can heal all wounds, inside and out. Jesus paid the price for our sins when he died on the cross, and because of him we can stand accepted before God. Jesus wants to have a relationship with you, and I believe he led you to me so I could introduce you to him. I can give you money to take with you to Mexico, but that will run out. A relationship with Jesus will never run out. He wants to go with you to Mexico and be with you always so that you can truly live and be free."

Rosa listened intently, nodding all the while. I continued, "It is really very easy to say yes to Jesus. The Bible says that if we confess our sins, Jesus is faithful and just to forgive our sins and cleanse us from all unrighteousness (1 John 1:9). So all you have to do is confess to him and tell Jesus you want to follow him daily…"

I was still talking when she interrupted. "*Sí*."

I broke off, confused. "Excuse me?"

"*Sí!* Yes!" she repeated eagerly. "I want to confess to Jesus now."

We ended up praying together, and Rosa accepted Jesus as her Lord and Savior. I gave her the audio-Bible, explaining that listening to God's Word every day would offer guidance and that if she prayed, God would be faithful to help her. I also explained how to find a true church that followed the Bible once she got home. There was so much to cover in so little time!

I was delighted with Rosa's decision as I left the room. But I was also conscious of how many trials and obstacles lay ahead for her. How would Rosa find the right church? Would she find any believers to encourage her? Would she get sidetracked with all her problems and give up on Jesus? What about this boyfriend of hers? What if he sold her audio-Bible to help pay for food?

I realized I needed to leave those worries on God's shoulders. After all, Rosa was his child. If God had guided her this far, including to our home where she could hear of Jesus, he would be faithful to continue guiding her. Instead, I shifted to offering praises of thanksgiving to God for bringing Rosa to himself.

That evening, we all climbed into our vehicle and drove Rosa and her children to the bus. All the way there, we continued assuring Rosa that, if she changed her mind, we would help her find a way to stay here legally where she could provide her children a great future here in the United States. She would just smile sweetly, never rejecting our offer but not agreeing with us either. It was clear she still wanted to go.

The bus arrived around 10:30 p.m. As Tim and I helped Rosa carry her belongings aboard the bus, I prayed that God would send a fellow passenger with compassion to help Rosa look after the children on such a long trip. As

Rosa hugged us goodbye, I also reminded her, "Once you leave, you can always call me, and I can pray for you. But I cannot help you anymore financially."

This was something God had convicted me to tell her as Tim and I did not want to create a dependency where we would be sending money with no accountability on her end. Rosa said she understood. Then I reached into my pocket for the money Tim and I had agreed together to give her. $800 wasn't much, but it was all we had, and it would at least get her home and started in her new life. Tim and I were both wiping our eyes as the bus drove off, touched by Rosa's sweet spirit and saddened to think of what she might face ahead.

Rosa called me when she got to Mexico. Someone had indeed reached out to her on that long trip and even held her baby so she could use the restroom. She thanked me and told me not to worry. Then my phone went silent.

I heard from Rosa one other time eight months later. She was calling on a pay phone from Mexico. Sobbing, she told me that her baby, now ten months old, was deathly sick. I could hear the baby screaming in the background. It broke my heart. While there was nothing I could do for her physically, I could pray for her, and I did so right there on the phone. I told her God would show her solutions. She wept intensely. The phone call ended with Rosa still crying uncontrollably. I hurt for her but felt that my hands were truly tied.

A few months later, I had a change of phone number. Since Rosa didn't have my new number, I knew I'd likely never hear from her again. It is unlikely I'll ever know this side of heaven the outcome of her situation either. But I feel privileged to have known Rosa and her family and continue to pray for her.

While Rosa had now left our home, the desire to do more and help others remained. Tim and I both felt more convinced than ever that God was calling us to foster and adopt. We went ahead and started the application process to be foster parents.

But remaining focused on that task would not prove easy. The doors didn't just fly open to make clear God's will. In fact, some doors would need to be pushed down and torn open. But what really stopped me too many times from going forward was not confusion about God's will but rather my own sealed door of fear.

From the Voice of Experience:

"I heard a quote from the child of a family who fosters, and he says it best: 'Mommy, kids are like paper airplanes. Foster kids are the airplanes that have been crumpled up and thrown in the trash. Foster families take those crumpled up airplanes and smooth them out so they can fly a little better.' So, go ahead, take a leap of faith and grab a crumpled-up airplane out of the trash and love those wrinkles out."
—L.W., a "Safe Family" foster and adoptive mom.

3 PERSISTENCE

Success is not final; failure is not fatal. It is the courage to continue that counts. —Winston S. Churchill

I believe a great, unseen battle occurs in the spiritual world when you decide to obey God. It doesn't matter what he tells you to do—whether to forgive a friend who has hurt you or a simple task like signing up for some classes. The apostle Paul once wrote to the church in Ephesus:

> "For our struggle is not against flesh and blood, but against the rulers, against the authorities, against the powers of this dark world and against the spiritual forces of evil in the heavenly realms." (Ephesians 6:12)

It is those spiritual forces of evil that fight to dissuade us, distract us, and discourage us from completing the mission God has given us. Something as simple as completing a nine-week Foster and Adoption Training Class can become such a thorn-patch of obstacles as to appear impossible.

The foster care system works through a two-tier structure where the mother company, the state-run Department of Children and Family Services, contracts private organizations to handle part of their case load. Many of these private entities have religious or denominational affiliation and can even pick what type of cases they want. But ultimately, all these sub-contractors are answerable to DCFS.

I chose to start directly with the Big Boss, DCFS, thinking this would open the door to more kids being placed with us, especially Spanish-speaking kids. The first step, even before taking classes, background checks, or medical reviews, was a home inspection. Here we ran into our first obstacle. The social worker sent out to inspect our home expressed great frustration with his journey. Our home was a full hour from the city where DCFS maintained its offices. The roads to get here were terrible. Our pond was too close to our home.

"You look like a great family with a lovely home," he summarized. "But the trip out here is too complicated. No caseworker will ever place a child with you because of all the trouble it would be to drop them off or pick them up. If you move closer to town, then maybe call us."

We could have taken his response as a closed door and given up on fostering. Instead, God led us to a church friend who was fostering a group of siblings through a private agency that was part of a Lutheran denomination. She talked to her caseworker about driving out to see if our home really was too far out in the countryside. With fewer foster parents and a lighter case load to place, this private agency had no objection to the distance involved in driving foster children out to our home. Even the concern over our pond was resolved by installing child-safety locks on all our doors. Now the only remaining obstacle standing in the way of children pouring into our home was the required foster parent training classes.

This wasn't the first time Tim and I had tried to sign up for the classes. Even with the greatest of intentions, we had always let other demands of life distract us from completing them. It didn't help that my husband is a farmer, and for him to take these classes entailed leaving weather-sensitive work, driving a full hour to sit through two more hours of class, then driving an hour home again.

It also meant finding someone to babysit our own two children for at least four hours each class session. The stress this put on Tim and me and the additional strain on our marriage was intense. But I had confidence that if God had called us to this task, he would provide a way. I didn't expect God to make everything smooth sailing, but I knew he would provide a way through the storm to reach the goal.

When I think of how we began our journey of fostering and adoption, I am reminded of the gospel account of the disciples caught in a storm on the Sea of Galilee when they spotted Jesus walking towards them across the storm-tossed waves:

> When the disciples saw him walking on the lake, they were terrified. "It's a ghost," they said, and cried out in fear. But Jesus immediately said to them: "Take courage! It is I. Don't be afraid." "Lord, if it's you," Peter replied, "tell me to come to you on the water." "Come," he said. Then Peter got down out of the boat, walked on the water and came toward Jesus. But when he saw the wind, he was afraid and, beginning to sink, cried out, "Lord, save me!" Immediately Jesus reached out his hand and caught him. "You of little faith," he said, "why did you doubt?" And when they climbed into the boat, the wind died down. Then those who were in the boat worshiped him, saying, "Truly you are the Son of God." (Matthew 14:26-33)

We see a lot of fear here in all of the disciples. Jesus comforts them, telling them to be brave. Then he calls them to come to him. But only *one* disciple has the courage to get out of the boat. This doesn't mean the disciples who stayed in the boat didn't love and believe in Jesus. The story ends with those in the boat worshipping Jesus and making a proclamation of faith that Jesus is the Son of God. But I believe that when Jesus issued his invitation to come, he was inviting all who were willing. Unfortunately, only Peter was willing to climb out of the boat and into the storm-tossed waves.

Likewise, when we make the choice to step out and meet Jesus where he has called us to "come," it can be downright scary. Many who truly love God will never have the courage to get out of the boat. When they encounter a closed door, they say, "God is not in this." They have the erroneous belief that if God has called them to a journey, he will make everything smooth sailing with all doors flying open before them.

When we study Scripture, we see just the opposite. Jesus called Peter to step out of the boat when the wind and waves were wild and crazy. He called Peter out of the boat when all that the disciples could see of Jesus through the storm was a blurry, nebulous image.

Similarly, when our future is unclear and the journey difficult, we have the choice to stay in a boat that is already being tossed and flooded by the storm or to step bravely into the storm to meet Jesus. Keep in mind that the safest place to be is with Jesus. As a fisherman, Peter recognized this. The disciples had been fighting the wind and waves all night long. Peter was tired of being unsuccessful in the boat. He knew that if Jesus commanded him to come, he would be safe.

We can ask God to make clear his will for our lives, but we must then be ready to move. The next step is ours to take. We can't just wait around for a calm, tranquil day to get out of the boat, or Jesus may have already passed us by, and our chance will be gone as it was for all the other disciples who stayed in the boat. Jumping out of the boat may be uncomfortable and take persistence, but we should love Jesus so much that we trust him to be the safest place in the world. And when we do, we will be a testimony to others of how our obedience led us to experience God's power of walking on the waves.

I have learned that when it comes to helping the parentless, homeless, or those otherwise in need, we should not expect a vacation on a sea of tranquility. Quite the contrary, we need to brace ourselves for some of the greatest adversity we have ever encountered. But never forget that if we dare to walk out onto the waves, Jesus will meet us there. He will not let us sink, and our faith will grow because we were willing to get out of the boat.

Still, as I mentioned earlier, it is important to keep in mind that not all doors will stand wide open, just waiting for us to walk through. Some doors we will have to push open in the name of our Savior and Lord. Tim and I quickly came to realize how persistent we'd have to be in pushing through doors if we were ever to become licensed foster parents. This included filling out reams of paperwork, going through background checks, fingerprinting, and another caseworker picking our home apart. We had to humble ourselves and allow the caseworker to tell us where and how we would need to change our living conditions.

All these things could have totally detoured us from continuing. Certainly, if we'd waited for God to calm the storm of life so that everything was easy and smooth, we'd never have jumped out of the boat. And we'd have lived out our lives with many regrets.

When God calls us to "come," to join him in some crazy, wind-blowing, lightning-crashing, wave-tossing adventure, we need to be like Peter. When I picture Peter getting out of the boat, I don't see him calculating the risks. I don't envision him looking left or right to judge the approval and support of his fellow disciples. I don't imagine Peter asking God to shine a beam of light down from heaven or some other sign as confirmation that Jesus actually invited him to come. Instead, I picture him as being so wildly enthusiastic to obey that he practically shoots out of the boat, his legs moving faster than his body, almost running across the waves to Jesus.

Of course, the passage goes on to tell us that as soon as Peter experienced the wind, he doubted and became afraid. But by now he was already committed. He spoke words we should all cry out when we are about to drown: "Help!"

I can identify with both Peter's impulsivity and his desire to be obedient. Much like Peter, I find myself in over my head, drowning in the responsibility of following Christ and failing to keep my eyes off the wind. A wind that seems unbearably fierce, violent, and more powerful than the One who called me out to come out into these very dangerous waves.

Indeed, the spiritual battle we face daily is fierce. If the devil can give us a good reason to quit before we ever begin, then we have accomplished nothing for the Kingdom and he has won. Before we'd ever met a real-life foster kid, Tim and I both talked constantly about quitting the classes. These centered around videos whose content was difficult to watch and digest. Fostering is not for the faint of heart, and I know we had to become aware that kids coming into our home might be from highly dysfunctional and abusive homes. But watching misbehavior, yelling, screaming, or any abuse reenacted on a TV screen is not a delightful experience.

Every class made us feel depressed and inadequate for the task ahead of us. I'd envisioned welcoming needy children into our home, but the class material made these children seem like little monsters. As we drove home, Tim and I would talk about giving up. Fear consumed our discussion. Maybe we were just not good enough. Tough enough. Equipped enough. Maybe we should leave fostering for some future date.

I should clarify that our teacher was amazing and remarkably experienced in fostering. She would often step outside of the class material to share her own firsthand experiences as a foster parent. Whether positive or negative, every story offered a glimmer of hope. Her instruction made a significant impact on our decision to continue the foster parenting process.

In November 2010, we finally finished our last class.

Our paperwork and medical evaluations were also now complete. But we hadn't yet told our family members about our plans to foster. Thanksgiving Day brought about that opportunity. As we enjoyed a sumptuous traditional Midwestern Thanksgiving dinner, a family member seated across from me embarked on the approximate following diatribe:

"I have no idea what their problem is! Why would people abandon their kids and not take care of them? Worse, why would anyone open up their home to those kids? It just enables the parents to keep sinning. They will never take responsibility if another person decides to do all the work for them. And what's really appalling is black kids being raised in a white home! It's just a crying shame! White needs to stay with white, and black with black."

Of course, I could not just sit there and keep eating. Calmly and quietly, I opened my big mouth. "That is exactly what Tim and I are about to do. We are now licensed and ready to be foster parents. Any day now we will receive a call to accept kids who cannot be raised by their parents. And I have been praying to God and have made clear to the fostering agency we will be excited and happy to have children who are of a different race than we are."

As all conversation broke off and everyone stared my way, Tim gave me his "you just had to do that!" face. To which I responded with my "of course!" face. I will admit I have not always been the humblest in my attitude along this journey. I truly believed I had to fight for righteousness and justice, and if that meant stepping on everybody in process, so be it.

I have since come to recognize we can waste a lot of energy and breath on people who can only be changed through prayer and through God's power. This wasn't the way I'd envisioned my family coming to know of our journey. I had wanted to paint a picture of how much God had blessed us and so in return we were willing to bless others. I'd wanted it to be a heroic picture. I'd wanted to receive praise and confirmation for our faithfulness to God.

Instead, the overall response from our extended family felt more like cold water to the face. Other God-fearing, church-attending acquaintances met our announcement with equally frigid rejoinders: "What about sexual abuse? Did it occur to you that the abused abuse others? What about your kids? You can do ministry after your kids are gone! Your kids should be your ministry. This is not going to end well!"

All words that generated so much fear. Unfortunately, they were also truthful words and well-intentioned. So where should we find a balance? How do you love when there is so much at risk? I had to turn to Scripture to defeat these blows. I would mentally recite one verse in particular:

> "There is no fear in love. But perfect love drives out fear . . . The one who fears is not made perfect in love. " (1 John 4:18)

Here is what I've come to learn from this scripture. Love cannot exist when fear reigns. Love is also more powerful than fear. Likewise, fear and faith do not mix. Fear is the opposite of faith. If we choose to allow love to take over our hearts and replace fear, we can experience a radical faith that can move mountains.

But our focus must be on love, not on the what-ifs. Another gospel account tells how Jesus helped a demon-possessed man (Mark 5). Astoundingly, once Jesus had transformed the man's life by casting out his demons, those who knew the man didn't respond in awe of the amazing power Jesus had just displayed. Instead, they responded with fear and begged Jesus to go away:

> "When they came to Jesus, they saw the man who had been possessed by the legion of demons, sitting there, dressed and in his right mind; and they were afraid . . . Then the people began to plead with Jesus to leave their region."
> (Mark 5:15;17)

Being afraid is rejecting God's power. Fear leads us away from Jesus. Nor can we rely on other people to guide us. Good people may lead us away from God's will for our lives because of fears they have not conquered within themselves. We need to drive out fear in the name of love. If we surrender to love, we can cast out all fear.

In time, Tim and I would witness our entire extended family come to accept our foster children as their own. In time, love would win over fear. God's blessings are contagious, and our own obedience to God despite fear would in time spread blessing throughout our extended family.

In fact, obeying God brings so many rewards. I believe one of those rewards Peter received for scrambling out of the boat is often overlooked. The passage in Matthew 14 tells us that after Peter doubted, he was immediately rescued by Jesus, who then walked back with Peter to the boat. It doesn't say Jesus carried Peter back. Nor did the storm go away until after they climbed into the boat. That means Peter walked beside Jesus back to the boat in the middle of a raging tempest.

Can you imagine what it was like to walk on the water alongside Jesus? That experience alone must have been worth the almost-drowning incident Peter had just faced. I don't ever want to miss out on the opportunity of walking with Jesus. I want to get out of the boat and follow his command. I know I won't do it perfectly, but hopefully if I start drowning, I will react like Peter and cry out to Jesus for help.

Through God's grace, we too can do what seems

impossible, like loving those who are not of our own genetic makeup, who may not look like us or act like us, but whom God has called into our lives for his purpose and for his praise. And just as we saw the other disciples respond when Peter returned with Jesus to the boat, the end result of our obedience will be praise and adoration to our Savior.

From the Voice of Experience:

"We were in church when we heard about how many kids in our own county are in need of foster care families. We sat down with our own biological sons (we have two) to see how they felt about this. They too were onboard with helping kids. So in 2011 we took classes to begin this journey. In November 2013, we received a call from our caseworker looking for a forever home for two girls, ages eighteen months and five years old. We went from a family of four to six overnight. It was and still is a great and remarkable journey. My husband and I can't imagine our lives any different. If you feel God tugging at your heart to become a foster or adoptive family for a child in need, please jump onboard. I guarantee you won't regret it!"
— C.B., a foster and adoptive mom.

4 THE CALL

As soon as I saw you, I knew an adventure was going to happen.—Winnie the Pooh

Three months had passed since we'd received our little piece of paper, i.e., a state license declaring our home and family a foster provider for children. But that's all we had. Just one little 4x6 piece of paper saying we were now foster parents. How could we be foster parents if we had yet to receive a single call regarding a foster child in need? My church friend who'd first put me in touch with this Lutheran agency had waited only two weeks to receive her first call for a placement of children into her home. But my phone remained silent.

The wait seemed forever, and doubts began to seize me. *What is taking so long? I thought there were a ton of kids out there needing a home! Why is our phone not ringing off the hook? Maybe that first social worker was right. Maybe we just aren't worthy of having kids placed in our home.*

As we waited, I prayed daily for those children God was preparing to enter our home. I prayed for our hearts and for our home, that we would be ready to receive and give. I knew God had all this under his control. But on many days my heart wavered, sinking into depression. *Maybe God's blessing is just not with us. Maybe we haven't been called and chosen to foster and adopt after all!*

During this period of waiting, my husband was offered a fabulous job in which he would be making more money and could work from home independently. This new job opportunity wasn't tied to the family agro-business, but was still in the field of agriculture, involving the sale of corn, wheat, and soybean seed in our local area. Tim would be able to make all his sales calls from home and only occasionally have to travel out-of-town to nearby Indiana.

At the time, I was so focused on my "why-not-right-now" questioning that it never occurred to me this new job opportunity had come from God exactly as we needed when we needed it. God was preparing our lives for a big shift, helping us get our home in order to receive foster children. Tim's support and presence at home would be essential to helping those new foster kids adjust.

My thoughts were so heavy at times, consuming a lot of my energy, that when the call finally did arrive, it took me completely by surprise. I was downstairs cleaning our basement, so my husband answered the phone. When Tim called down to me that Social Services was on the phone, I couldn't believe it.

"Really?" I demanded skeptically. "Don't kid with me on this!"

But when I rushed upstairs, it was indeed a social worker on the phone. They had two children needing foster placement. Would we be willing to take them?

"Yes, yes!" I responded without hesitation. In my excitement, I didn't ask any details other than the children's names, when they would be coming, and what might be their favorite toy or gift. I had no idea why the children had been placed into foster care, nor did I ask. All that mattered is that we were getting some children to bless.

I also didn't ask if they were adoptable. In my naivety, I assumed they were, since we'd listed "foster-to-adopt" when filling out our paperwork. We'd also listed that we only wanted children younger than our own birth kids. I later learned that what we'd filled out on our paperwork hadn't even been taken into consideration in this placement.

Tim and I were so excited. The call came on a Friday, and the children would be arriving on Monday. They were currently living with their grandparents, and the social worker was giving them time to collect their belongings and say goodbye. The parents had been neglectful because of drug and alcohol abuse, so the grandparents had gained custody. But Grandma hadn't been abiding by agency rules. She couldn't be firm enough with the parents and kept allowing them access to the kids even when they were still doing drugs. Social Services felt the children weren't being protected and cared for, so they had removed them to a non-relative foster care placement. I asked no prying questions except how to make the children feel at home in our household.

Since the children's real names cannot be disclosed, let's call them T-Man and Kay-Kay. T-Man was a five-year-old boy, Kay-Kay a three-year-old girl. Each was exactly eight months younger than my own birth son and daughter. That meant I would now have in our home two five-year-old boys, a four-year-old girl, and a three-year-old girl.

Briefly, and I mean ever so briefly, the caseworker also rattled off that T-Man had Cerebral Palsy. His main symptoms were a limp and difficulty using his right hand. Then in a hurried dismissal, she finished, "But it's so mild; I can't even tell."

To be truthful, I was so excited I didn't really consider what problems the children might have. Nor did I have any idea what Cerebral Palsy entailed. I trusted with all my heart that our agency knew what we could and could not handle. So I listened half-heartedly to this description of mild CP, believing in my heart that God could transform any and all situations. After all, I had God on my side. What else mattered?

That very night we prepared the rooms and gifts for the children's arrival. The excitement in our home was glorious. Some church friends pitched in to provide brand-new twin beds for the kids. Other friends gave me bags of clothes for the kids. My house was already overflowing with the blessings of having said "yes".

February 8, 2011, is a date forever sealed in our hearts

and memories. When Monday finally arrived, our joy was just bubbling over. It is hard to contain the happiness one feels about being able to bless another person by sharing everything you have. However, we were also conscious that our increase meant their loss. While we were excited to add to our family, our new foster children would be losing everything they'd ever known. I prayed that God would prepare their hearts and guide us in compassion.

T-Man and Kay-Kay ended up arriving a full hour earlier than the caseworker had told us to expect them. But we were more than ready, and they were so precious. I loved them the moment I saw them. I knew they were mine, chosen by God. Kay-Kay let me unbuckle her and lift her out of the car seat. T-Man held my hand until we were inside. Our birth son and daughter, Caleb and Faith, also ran immediately out of the house to greet them.

"It's like Christmas!" Faith announced. "Come see all your gifts."

Her usual bubbly self, Faith immediately set about helping Kay-Kay not to be scared. Caleb in turn was reserved but sweet, helping T-Man open all his gifts. I just stood back and watched. It was amazing. *This is why Jesus says we should be like little children,* I realized, *ready to love, easy to love.*

Kay-Kay melted our hearts, being a beautiful, clever little girl. She had slightly wavy but tangled long, brown hair. Her bangs were very much overgrown, covering her eyes. Thin and wiry, she had energy for two people, talking constantly and never sitting still.

As for T-Man, the caseworker was right that his handicap wasn't really noticeable. He did have trouble using his right hand, but compensated for it by using his left hand. His right leg had a slight limp, and his mouth slanted downward on the right side of his face. Later we discovered he was completely deaf in his right ear, something of which neither his parents, grandparents, nor his caseworker had any idea.

It took multiple medical exams by specialists before we found out that the right side of T-Man's brain was damaged, either from birth or at two years of age when he had a seizure and stopped breathing due to an untreated fever of 104.5. We also discovered from his birth records that T-Man had failed his post-natal hearing exam, but no one had bothered to look further into it. Either way, the right side of his body had been left permanently damaged.

The children came with just one trash bag of clothes mixed with toys between the two of them. Kay-Kay's only pair of shoes were snow boots. Most of the clothes were youth size 9. I wondered if Grandma had just thrown random items into the bag, thinking they would soon be coming back, or if this was really all they had. It didn't seem possible all their belongings could fit into one bag. As for their few toys, these were inexpensive, dirty, and mostly broken.

T-Man's and Kay-Kay's parents had been arrested and charged with child neglect resulting from their own heroin abuse. For years before the parents lost custody, the children had a disrupted childhood of missed meals, inconsistent care, and above all, love. These scars would take years to undo. But God had brought them to the right home. We were so ready to care for them.

However, we were also well aware that our foster parent journey would necessitate multiple dental surgeries, physical therapy, counseling, hearing tests, all of them located at least two hours from our home. T-Man's and Kay-Kay's state-provided insurance only covered actual appointments and surgeries, so gas and mileage would be completely out of our own pocket.

On the first day of introductions, the social workers stayed with us for an hour. They were supportive, and everything went so smoothly. If ever I was fearful, I'd been so wrong to be so. I knew that God had been speaking to me all last week about not being afraid. He knew all along there was nothing to fear, as the apostle Peter assures in one of his epistles:

> "Who is going to harm you if you are eager to do good? But even if you should suffer for what is right, you are blessed. Do not fear their threat; do not be frightened." (1 Peter 3:13-17, NLT)

By the afternoon, T-Man had grown really attached to the toys we'd given him. Our choice of gifts turned out to be truly guided by God. That same day before T-Man and Kay-Kay arrived, I'd just cruised through Wal-Mart, picking out clothing, toys, and other items and placing them in the cart. The final bill had just about blown us over, but every gift, even the new Toy Story underwear turned out to be just perfect for their needs. They didn't even bother playing with the toys they'd brought but clung literally to the new ones.

> *A Tip for Foster Parents: Appropriate gifts waiting for the children when they arrive is one indispensable way to make them feel at home.*

For aspiring foster or adoptive parents reading this, let me just emphasize the indispensable benefits I've discovered in having gifts waiting for the children when they arrive. Underwear, toothbrushes, hair brushes, new clothes, and new toys are essentials.

I wish I'd thought of shoes too. Considering the children were from our same area, it hadn't occurred to me they would arrive without shoes and clothes to match our current weather. How on earth had they made it this far? We couldn't even go outside and play because the kids didn't have the right kind of clothes and shoes for Illinois in February, which was unbearably cold the day they arrived, even if we had no snow. I was already mentally planning a midnight shopping spree once the children were asleep.

When supper time rolled around, Tim baked a pizza. The moment the family was called to eat, T-Man was up in his chair, waiting. I always try to keep fruit on our table at all times. That night I had grapes, cherries, and one plum. T-Man and Kay-Kay didn't want to even try the pizza. They wanted fresh food, in this case, grapes. That is all Kay-Kay ate, grape after grape.

T-Man did eventually eat his slice of pizza, then asked for grapes. Once he'd eaten those, he asked for more. Then he asked to try the bigger "grapes". I explained that these were actually cherries and had a seed in them. Once Caleb showed T-Man how to eat them, T-man happily devoured the cherries. Then he asked to try the biggest "grape", i.e., the plum, which he absolutely loved.

We quickly noticed that Kay-Kay would try nothing new, but T-Man would try anything. He was incredibly thin but must have had a huge metabolism because he sure could pack away a lot of food in that tiny tummy of his. Over the coming days, Tim and I found ourselves baffled. Here were two kids born in the USA and who'd lived to this point just an hour from our home. Yet they'd never eaten corn-on-the-cob, plums, or cherries.

And we were the lucky ones who got to watch their eyes light up as they discovered new foods. That first evening, T-Man didn't want me to take his plate away even when he was too full to eat anymore. He'd piled it with bunches of grapes, three cherries, a half-eaten plum, and another piece of pizza just in case he got hungry later. He was used to planning for the future when no food might be available.

Meanwhile, Kay-Kay was already down from her chair, playing again. After supper, Tim chased all the kids around the house in an endless game of tag. Caleb drifted off to play tractors, alone in his own world. It was precious to see Kay-Kay run two circles around him, then touch his arm and demand, "Chase me!" As she ran away, Caleb jumped up from his tractors to chase her. Laughter filled our home. That moment felt like God's will. Laughter, surely, must be a sign of God's will being completed!

Then T-Man grabbed a toy gun from Caleb's toy chest. Laughing as he chased Tim with the gun, he called out, "I'm gonna shoot your ass!"

Tim immediately stopped. He smiled because you couldn't help but smile at T-Man's innocence, then managed to get out in a feeble voice, "Um, nice words, Buddy!"

This probably made no sense to T-Man, who went on to say a good many more vulgar words. Fortunately, he had a small speech impediment which made it hard to really understand him. I had been praying for a long time that God would place a shield around these children, and I realized that his inability to speak clearly was in itself such a shield. It was also a shield that God was placing around Caleb and Faith to protect them from understanding such vulgar words. We had full confidence that after a few weeks in our home those words would be gone from T-Man's vocabulary.

A surprising thing happened that night even before we'd put the children to bed. When T-Man and Kay-Kay first arrived at our home, we introduced ourselves to them as Bess and Tim. We didn't anticipate how quickly they would adopt us into their hearts. Walking into the kitchen where Tim and I were cleaning up from dinner, Kay-Kay demanded happily, "*Daddy*, chase me!"

My heart jumped at her words. By evening, T-Man and Kay-Kay were both calling us Daddy and Mommy. We heard only one mention of their real daddy when Kay-Kay pointed at a set of buck antlers mounted on a wall and announced that her daddy had one too. Beyond that, Kay-

Kay only mentioned her grandma while T-Man didn't mention his birth family at all.

I have since talked to many foster parents who also have birth children in the home. I've learned that it is very natural for foster kids to appear to adapt quickly. It is part of their survivor instinct. However, I was so new at this foster experience that I took their calling us Mommy and Daddy as their acceptance of us in their hearts.

Unfortunately, the journey is much more complicated than a simple descriptive term of daddy or mommy. T-Man and Kay-Kay would need to learn a totally different role of authority and care that a mother and father are supposed to provide for their children. Establishing boundaries and rules in love would drive me over the edge at times. I would feel like a complete failure, and I would have the desire to give up. But I would also learn to appreciate the hugs and kisses, and my heart would continue to jump every time they called me *Mommy*.

From the Voice of Experience:

"My stomach had butterflies jumping all around inside of me as I anticipated meeting these children of total strangers. I was about to share everything I ever had and loved with them—even my own birth children and their rooms and their things. Fear mixed with excitement, a strange combination, yet I could feel God's peace. All my worries vanished when they arrived and I could see their faces light up with excitement and joy about the simple things our family had taken for granted: warm food, fresh fruits and vegetables, a bath filled with bubbles and toys, a bed all for themselves to sleep on, clean clothes, siblings who can teach them so much, a mommy who would respond to their worries, and a daddy who would protect them from danger. I remember watching them as they slept peacefully in

our home that first night when they arrived. He breathes, free of any disturbance. So does she with a quiet contentment. My heart also rests. My children are finally home."
—M. L., foster parent.

5 THE WAKE-UP CALL

The kids who need the most love will ask for it in the most unloving ways.—Anonymous

The honeymoon stage didn't last long. One week, to be exact. After that week, it was like a bomb went off in the house. The day the agency brought T-Man and Kay-Kay to my home, they'd told me these kids were 90% adoptable. They'd also said both parents were in distant drug rehab centers.

So why would they be calling me to schedule a parental visit within days after the children arrived? Why would anyone in their right mind take a child to a drug center for a visit? How safe is a center full of recovering addicts? Wouldn't the parents be going through withdrawal? Where would the children visit with parents? Why did the agency want these children to relive their abuse by even seeing their parents? Shouldn't the agency wait until the parents are completely healed instead of pushing for a visit this quickly?

Apart from all these worrisome questions churning over and over in my mind, T-Man's and Kay-Kay's mounting misbehavior was beginning to overwhelm me. One day while at the store, T-Man ran away from me. How do you shop and watch four preschoolers at the same time when one of them dashes away? What is the first thing you do? Do you leave three to find the one? And yes, Jesus's parable of the one lost sheep (Luke 15:3–7) did enter my mind. And, no, I had no desire to leave my other "ninety-nine" to go find the single rebellious one.

Though in the end that's exactly what I did do! Taking my shopping cart and my other three little ones to the cash register, I begged the cashier to please watch them for me.

Luckily, the store wasn't busy, and the cashier was kind enough to agree, so I sprinted off, looking for Mr. T-Man. And boy, was I mad! I think you could have seen fumes rising from my nose. I searched every aisle and could not find him. Before panic set in, I lowered myself to bribery.

"Come out wherever you are, T-Man," I shouted out, "and I will let you watch Toy Story in the car."

We had a DVD player in our vehicle, and T-Man had already learned its entertainment value. Immediately a little face popped out from the very last aisle of the store, where T-Man had hidden by squeezing in behind some furniture. He had a huge smile and kept laughing like a maniac. How should I discipline this child for running away? I'd never had to do that with my children. I ended up treating him to his Toy Story just like I had said and put off disciplining for another day.

To add to the increased stress of managing their discipline, the agency called with so many requests. Get the kids in school now. Attend all school-parent meetings. Schedule dentist appointments. Sign T-Man up for physical therapy. The grandmother had checked a box on their health forms, indicating T-Man and Kay-Kay both had tuberculosis, so now I had to go get chest X-rays for each of them.

I was overwhelmed, to say the least. When the parents had lost custody to the grandmother, she had clearly done the absolute minimum to care for them. I was amazed at how neither child's teeth had ever been cared for. Both had numerous blackened, rotted teeth with huge holes in their molars and front teeth. Here in Illinois, healthcare and dental care are free for the homeless and poor. So what kind of grandmother doesn't take her own grandkids to a free dental checkup?

Not only that, Grandma had them in her care for a whole year under the agency's careful monitoring. Why had the agency not required her to care for their teeth, physical therapy, doctor visits, or at the least, enroll T-Man and Kay-Kay in preschool, a free service provided for foster children through Social Services? I was scrambling to undo years of neglect while the agency kept pressuring me to do it more quickly. But why hadn't they pushed for these same requirements while the children were under Grandma's care? It would have saved me a lot of stress and would have helped her own grandkids so much if she would have been required to do more than just feed the kids. The stark difference with which the agency treats a family-relation foster home as opposed to a non-familial home is unfair for the children. This kind of neglect should have never made it past the agency's supposedly watchful eye! I quickly learned that even if you asked questions, the answers supplied weren't always truthful. In time, unanswered questions became the norm.

The Social Services agency had set up an IEP (Individualized Education Program) meeting because both kids were significantly behind educationally. I was taken aback by how much work had to be done just to get them enrolled in school before the IEP meeting: dentist check-ups, medical physicals, and tons of paperwork. My head was spinning. I questioned whether I could handle all the responsibility and requirements.

The IEP meeting was also scheduled without asking me about my own schedule, and I was expected to go to that, too. How would I get all these check-off items done while managing all four kids? I didn't have a regular babysitter for my two birth kids. The agency expected immediate compliance, but keeping watch over four preschoolers while filling out paperwork in some government office terrified me.

To make matters even more intense, the night before the IEP meeting Faith started throwing up uncontrollably. Tim stayed home with the other kids while I rushed Faith to the ER in town. She could not stop throwing up, her stomach bloated to the point that I could not bend her to carry her in. She was vomiting so much so fast that the ER doctor called for an immediate ambulance ride to the children's hospital in St. Louis, Missouri, an hour's drive from our home. Faith was given morphine to calm her incessant pain and crying.

It was a heartbreaking night. The next morning, my husband arranged for a babysitter to stay with the three kids at home and drove to switch places with me at the hospital so I could go to the IEP meeting. I really didn't know if I could continue down this road.

We eventually discovered that Faith was just experiencing an unusual virus, so uncommon the hospital placed her in isolation for a twenty-four hour observation period before releasing her to go home. Was it just coincidence that this was the night before the IEP meeting? Or did the devil have a hand in this fresh and inconvenient family crisis?

A dear friend volunteered to come with me to the IEP meeting. Her support was incredibly vital to the success of our meeting. A school teacher herself, she knew that sometimes in an IEP meeting the special needs of foster kids could be overlooked, unintentionally or intentionally, due to the tendency for foster children to be constantly moved around. Truthfully, who wants to invest time, effort, and money into kids who at any given time could move away to become some other school's problem? My friend's knowledge and experience would help me understand what I was about to hear and how to best advocate for my foster children.

At the IEP meeting, I learned for the first time the intimate details of our case. I am sure it was not the intention of the supervisor chairing the meeting to surprise me. I am sure he assumed I knew exactly how my children got into foster care. Well, I did not! I'd trusted the agency to tell me whatever they felt I needed to know. In a matter-of-fact voice, he read the following horrifying story, which I will try to summarize, as an introduction of the children's case to the others in attendance.

Two years ago in February, a woman had called 911 to report a passed-out man on her neighbor's porch. When police officers entered the neighbor's home, they found drug paraphernalia, trash bags everywhere, broken glass, mice crawling around, passed-out adults throughout the house, and two small children, ages three years and eighteen months. The fridge held nothing but beer to drink and a small block of molding cheese.

Social Services removed the two children from the home, placing them in the custody of their grandparents. But the grandfather was quite ill, on oxygen, and unable to move much. This left the children's care to their grandmother, who had not attended any previous IEP meetings and proved incapable of enforcing Social Services regulations.

These included strict orders not to allow the birth parents near their children outside of supervised visits. And then visits could only happen if they were sober and clean. On a random inspection visit, the caseworker witnessed all parties involved breaking the rules. A week later, the children were removed for placement in a non-familial foster home.

In an IEP, the law requires everyone present to create a tailored plan with certain goals to be met within a certain time frame. Each teacher, parent, and child must meet the standards set at the meeting. If I hadn't gone to this meeting, I would have been uninformed of the details regarding my involvement and the kids would have had no advocate.

Sending T-Man and Kay-Kay to the local preschool would not satisfy the children's IEP goals. T-Man was behind in every category possible. Kay-Kay had attention problems. The goals for her included learning how to control impulses, sit still for lessons, and learn basic songs along with the standard ABCs and numbers. But the school system in my district where I pay my taxes had no space available for foster kids with severe learning behaviors.

By this point in the IEP meeting, I was a wreck and in tears. I was now learning just how my foster children had ended up in state care, and the images of a handicapped three-year-old trying to find something to feed his crying baby sister or the two of them scrambling through broken glass and dirty syringes left me in deep distress. My friend was trying to console me even as the various teachers and superintendent debated where to send my kids. The final conclusion was for T-Man and Kay-Kay to be enrolled in a local Head Start program until they could be transitioned into our area's school district. I agreed and promised to do my part, i.e., attend all required meetings and make sure the children didn't miss school.

One reason my friend was so vital in that meeting was that, while I was crying, it was her voice of reason that prompted the decision to place T-Man and Kay-Kay locally. The original suggestion had been to enroll them in a Behaviorally Disordered (BD) preschool that had some openings, which would necessitate an hour's ride each way in a private van. I had made it clear I believed that kind of environment would be detrimental to my foster children's success, especially since their IEP paperwork didn't list any behavioral problems.

That was when my friend spoke up to mention how important it was to keep the children close to home. She also brought up the urgency of minimizing the trauma of a new environment by avoiding long daily car rides. She pointed out that the best teachers for T-Man and Kay-Kay would be the example of my own birth kids as opposed to being surrounded on a daily basis by disruptive, non-verbal BD preschoolers.

> *A Tip for Foster Parents: Don't go at it alone. Find a friend or friends willing to commit to walking this foster journey with you and to be on call when you need an ally at your side.*

I am still very grateful to this friend. Every person who goes into the journey of fostering should make sure to have a friend like this. It's not just having a shoulder to cry on. It's having a friend who isn't scared to speak up on your behalf when you as a new foster parent feel paralyzed due to the complexity of foster care issues.

We ended up finishing out that school year in the local Head Start program. It proved a good transition for T-Man and Kay-Kay. They only had to attend a few hours every day, and they were placed in the program together. The teachers were kind and understanding about their situation. When they graduated, we threw a family party to celebrate.

Their attendance at Head Start also gave me a few hours each day to spend with my own children. I felt we were constantly driving to therapy or school, with my children having to sit for hours in waiting rooms for therapy or other services for the foster kids. Not only did my children have to share their mother and her affection with their new foster siblings, but my children now had a stressed-out mom who was constantly trying to juggle pleasing the agency and meeting countless appointments and goals.

For this reason, those few daily hours of Head Start became precious to me. I needed time just to laugh and play with my own kids. And healthy as they were compared to the many needs of our foster kids, my own kids still needed their mommy. Kids grow up so fast, and I regret now not shutting my phone off completely or using those hours to cook or clean instead of being more intentional in paying attention to Caleb and Faith.

Of course, I had expected things would settle down as time progressed. T-Man and Kay-Kay were in school. T-Man was also in intensive physical therapy for his Cerebral Palsy, and monthly dentist visits were gradually fixing the multiple cavities and rotten teeth. But of course, things did not settle down.

I'd left that first IEP with many questions for the children's caseworker. She explained in detail about the parents' addiction to heroin and that the chance of recovering from such addiction was only 1%. To me, this meant that within a short few months, our foster kids would be adoptable. I now know, as does anyone who has ever started the process of fostering to adopt, that this is never the case. In Illinois, the average foster child is stuck in the system for five years. That's the average. Which means some kids are stuck in the system for many, many more years.

At the time, I was so new to the process that I was caught off guard when the social worker called to say we needed to start visits with birth parents. I'd only had the kids for a few days when I received this call. I was dumbfounded. Not only were these small kids being required to see their parents, bringing back traumatizing memories of neglect and abuse, but they would have to be transported to the parents' physical location. The birth father was a full hour away in a drug rehabilitation facility. The mother was in another rehab center two hours away in the opposite direction.

To make matters worse, since the grandparents had "bonded" with the children during their year of custody, we were required to work in grandparent visits too. The stress of managing three family visits in one week, Head Start, physical therapy, dental care, Social Services visits to my house to make sure I was abiding by their rules, while working time into the schedule for our own family events and children was pushing me over the brink. Social workers would show up at our home at least four times a week. The stress of keeping our home spotless and the children perfectly well-behaved and not fighting became overwhelming.

> *A Tip for Foster Parents: Neither you, your kids, nor your home needs to be perfect, so just relax and enjoy the mess!*

Looking back, I realized I should have just relaxed. Kids fight. Kids make messes. Oh, well! But I wanted to be that picture-perfect foster parent because I thought my testimony as a Christian was on constant trial. Weren't Christians supposed to be extraordinary role models? Exceptional parents? Isn't a clean and tidy house a sign of a diligent and dedicated follower of Christ?

Not only was the stress taking a toll on me, but Tim's new job was making demands on him. He needed quiet office time, which he wasn't getting with a houseful of kids. All this tension started eating into our marriage. In my journal, I wrote:

Yesterday was a freaky day. So I chugged the Coke in the fridge. And, yes, I admit, Tim and I had a bad argument. Something we are ashamed of—and right in front of the kids. The devil soon lied to us: "What good are you? This is the environment they came from! How are you any better?" Such a lie! Such discouragement. When it was time to go to bed, T-Man and Kay-Kay had a big-time meltdown, screaming, kicking, throwing things. It was a nightmare. I had to comfort each for a long time. At the same time, I had no arms left to comfort my own children. I watched Caleb's and Faith's sad and confused eyes as I cradled the "misbehaved" children in my arms and neglected them. In tears and extreme exhaustion, I retreated to bed.

Another morning, I started my journal with a prayer:

> *"God, send me some message saying this is truly what You wanted!"* Our devotions today were spot-on. Mine was mostly the message on God's provision: my help coming from God. But Tim's devotional from Henry Blackaby made me bawl. *"Love brings Obedience"* was the title. *"Genuine love for God leads to wholehearted obedience".* Even when things are tough. Even when they don't make sense to us right now. I know this is His will—walk—no matter what may happen. And don't give up!

I continued writing in my journal about how much disobedience I was getting from T-Man. He was constantly having melt-downs, kicking, screaming, and throwing himself into tantrums in any location, whether at the doctor's office, parking lot, or playground. These occurred especially when I asked him to stop what he was doing in order to transition into another event such as getting into the car.

At the same time, my son Caleb, who had been battling ear infections since a toddler, was prescribed antibiotics. My journal chronicles his allergic reaction to the medicine and how his body swelled with black and blue bruises from hives. He had a tough time walking and couldn't touch things. Even his lips were swollen. So I had one five-year-old with drastic behavior problems and another who was sick, demanding attention and care, all the while my own energy was draining.

On the bright side, T-Man and Kay-Kay were experiencing some of their "firsts" with us as well as experiencing country life. Once a day we would go on an adventure in the woods behind our house. The crisp air and birds chirping would sweep away my stress and burdens. Outdoors, the kids seemed free, their misbehaviors so much less. There was nothing to fight over. Sticks, trees, leaves to collect, even animal tracks were all stimulating and brought us great delight.

My mother brought many toys, fruit, and words of reassurance. She hadn't been so keen originally on the fostering idea, but now she gave me constant support in the midst of the hardest days. I remember her comforting me one day when Kay-Kay fell down, quickly developing a bruise. I was in a panic over whether I'd be accused of abuse by the agency or whether the birth dad would notice and demand the children be removed from our home. Mom encouraged me not to be scared. She pointed out how our foster kids felt that they belonged in my house. That knowledge should help me walk confidently.

Sometimes in my journal, I would note that as night came and our home slept, I found peace. To be perfectly honest, I was surviving in those days on hope and peace. Hope that tomorrow would be better and that once everyone was asleep, peace would be found.

When you bring children into your home from a totally different background, you should expect some turmoil as you all adjust to living together. One must plan for larger meals, more laundry, more messes in the home and car, and even additional time to get everyone ready. Such seemingly trivial things are a difficult adjustment when your family has been added to so suddenly.

But for such adjustments, I do believe I was ready. What I found more difficult was how much of a struggle it was for our new children to adapt to our current family schedule and lifestyle. T-Man and Kay-Kay desperately needed a consistent schedule and daily routines. But they also fought against those routines. They constantly challenged my authority.

A Tip for Foster Parents: If available, regular scheduled counseling/therapy for the entire foster family is invaluable throughout the foster care journey.

I've come to believe strongly that every foster parent and foster child would be better served if therapy is provided throughout the entire foster care process. If I as an adult found it a struggle to modify my life and expectations to accommodate more children, how is a child supposed to know how to deal with all the emotions and changes that come with acquiring a new family? The agency explains absolutely nothing to the children as though a child is resilient and can handle any change. Likewise, a foster parent is told only what the agency deems they should know. It's like trying to piece together a puzzle while missing a majority of the pieces.

This in turn requires a constant balancing act of trying to regulate your emotions and keep them hidden so you can focus your love and care for the children. My most disheartening moment came through the children's social worker. I had prayed that God would somehow cancel the visits to their parents' drug rehab facilities. I truly expected God to answer this prayer request. With Almighty God on my side, we would not have to do the normal, dreaded fostering task of parental visits. God would deliver us from them all.

So, I was truly shocked when the caseworker actually did show up to take the kids for their first visit. I really believed in the power of prayer and that it would change the course of the visit. Maybe the dad would cancel. Maybe the courts would see the futility of such a visit and prohibit it.

But it appeared all my prayers had been useless. The caseworker informed us that a woman who drove for Social Services would be picking up T-Man and Kay-Kay on Monday to visit their father. This involved an hour's drive, an hour's visit, then an hour's return drive. I just couldn't comprehend the logic behind a visit with a dad who had not protected his children and even now might not be stable. What kind of issues would I have to deal with after such a visit?

I recognized by this point that the agency would not offer me any kind of help. I would once again be left to pick up the pieces of this broken situation and try to mend them as best as I could. Which wasn't much due to my own inexperience in helping traumatized children.

Foster parents need to realize that their home may be beautiful and able to meet a child's physical needs, but it will still feel alien and foreign to a traumatized child. In my naivety, I believed my love, care, and the material things I provided were enough to heal all wounds. Plus, I had on my side the power of the Living God, so I believed I could handle any situation. Instead, every day brought new challenges for which I was unprepared. Among the biggest of those challenges were the parental visits.

From the Voice of Experience:

"I'm scared. Scared to complain about being disrespected as a foster parent. Scared because the people disrespecting me are the people in charge of our case and can ultimately make moves to take our foster daughters out of our home. I feel intimidated. I feel like I have no choice in the matter. I don't get to decide if adding an extra hour to today's visit is workable for us. It doesn't matter what plans we had, the girls will be home an hour later than expected. The three-year old who cried this morning because she didn't want to miss her swimming lesson to go on this visit has no choice either. I'm tired. Tired of this consuming my life. I feel hopeless. Hopeless to help these girls find a stable, loving home that can be theirs forever. No one else seems to care about the girls' best interest. Everyone seems to have an agenda and boxes they have to check off."

—A.G., foster mom.

6 VISITS

Because what makes you a man is not the ability to make a child, it's the courage to raise one.—President Barak Obama

Every foster parent can tell you that visiting days are some of the toughest. These days not only add significant stress to the foster parent, but both birth and foster children also feel the stress. For the foster family, each visit involves re-experiencing a cycle of emotions that goes something like this:

Tension planning the visit: There is never a perfect time for a visit. It usually occurs during nap time or after school, or the drive to the birth parents' location falls over a meal time. The tension begins when the social worker calls or texts to say the birth parents are requesting a visit, which is their legal right. The visit is typically scheduled according to the convenience of the birth parent. The social worker must then do whatever is necessary to accommodate their request. This often includes providing transportation for the birth parent or giving them gas money to drive to a designated location. Unless the parents are in rehab or jail, in which case the children are automatically brought to them.

In scheduling such visits, the child's own schedule or routine is not considered. If a foster child refuses to visit their parents, they are not given a choice. So the tension begins usually the day before a visit when the child's caseworker informs the foster parent, "We are on for a visit tomorrow." Many times, it's hit and miss. If the birth parent doesn't call in by a certain time, they miss their chance for a visit that week.

Transportation to the visits: Since birth parents may be in rehab, prison, or trying to start a new life somewhere, the distance to parental visits can be significant, especially in rural America. For our foster children's birth mother, the rehab center was two hours away. That made for a very long and stressful round trip for T-Man and Kay-Kay. I would always pack a good-sized bag with plenty of snacks and things for the kids to do during their trip. The Social Services transporter always thanked us appreciatively since this made the journey a far more pleasant one for both the children and driver.

The visits: Visits are initially supervised by the transporter. These are typically one hour a week for each parent. Grandparents and siblings can sometimes petition for visits as well. If the parents show progress over time, supervised visits of one hour are increased to unsupervised visits of three hours. These unsupervised visits can be a difficult strain on the foster family. If the birth parent is not in rehab or incarcerated, they can take the children anywhere they want and do whatever they want with the kids. For the foster parents, this is a grueling experience that necessitates total surrender to God and trust in his protection. If the visits have progressed this far, the agency assumes the parent is ready to be responsible without supervision.

The trip home: The transporter may have to deal with major misbehavior on the return trip. A DVD player can be an invaluable saving grace. We had one in our own vehicle and discovered it to be an excellent distraction, especially after the raw emotions of a parental visit. Such visits could also be exhausting for the children, and on many occasions our foster children would just sleep all the way home.

Regression: Foster parents should expect regression

once the children are back home where they feel safe to let down barriers and express certain emotions. If we as adults can find it a challenge to make sense of the emotions after such a visit, how much more so for a child trying to manage the raw feelings of neglect, anger, memories of past abuse, grief, and confusion about their future. Behavior for T-Man and Kay-Kay was always terrible after visits. It took us almost a year to find a way to deal with these days. We did so by planning a party of celebration for their return home instead of just dreading that moment.

Fretting over the when, where, and how of the next visit: Since this cycle just keeps repeating, it adds enormous tension to a foster care family. My advice to myself and to others going through this journey is to take one visit at a time. Just think about the visit currently before you. And always pray, intentionally putting aside the cycle of worry. After all, your dread and worries about this particular visit may not even happen. It is truly a waste of emotion and energy to worry about things over which we have no control.

I remember only too well the first time our foster children had to leave for their visit, this one was with their birth father. It seemed weird that a total stranger labeled "the transporter" would be arriving to take them. Since the children had never met her, this disturbed them. For the agency's caseworkers, visits become completely matter-of-fact. But for me and the foster children, this "transporter" was a new face with a new purpose.

Meanwhile, T-Man did not want to go see his daddy. He insisted his home was with us. It took a lot of talking and reassurance on my part to coax him into going. Once they'd left, I began thinking of all the Bible verses I'd memorized about deliverance, rescuing, and vindication. I prayed that God would make these verses ring true for our own situation. One passage especially became stamped on my heart:

> "How long will you defend the unjust and show partiality to the wicked? Defend the weak and the fatherless; uphold the cause of the poor and the oppressed. Rescue the weak and the needy; deliver them from the hand of the wicked." (Psalm 82:2-4)

I wanted the Bible to come alive in our lives as foster parents. I also believed wholeheartedly that God would relieve me and our foster children from having to deal with these visits. So I felt confused as to why God was not rescuing them as I thought he should. I was sure God would prevent them from seeing their "other daddy" as we had been calling him.

I was interpreting the scriptures I'd memorized to read as I wanted. I assumed the "other daddy" was the "wicked" referenced in the above passage, while the "fatherless" were our foster children due to the abuse and lack of parental protection they'd suffered. I arrogantly expected the way God would "deliver" them would be to remove them permanently out of their broken home and place them swiftly and smoothly in our own home.

But God's ways are not my ways. And even when I don't understand, God does. I knew God was working, but I felt frustrated with his timing, and I spoke very candidly with him about it. I remember constantly asking God "why" and not in a very kind way either. Years later, I would understand how vital these visits were to the reunification of our foster children with their birth parent. God does see the future. But knowing God knows the future doesn't necessarily make the present any easier.

After that first visit, T-Man showed the worst signs of regression. At five years old, he had been potty-trained for years according to the caseworker. But that evening, he pooped in the bath. He also had two pee accidents during the day, a clear indication of regression. When bedtime came, he started a temper tantrum of screaming, moaning, kicking, and scratching his arm until it was bright red. Tim would remove his hand, then he'd go right back to scratching.

"People do this!" T-Man insisted when Tim remonstrated with him. "People scratch themselves. I see them do this."

He was right, of course. Heroin addicts are known for "skin picking". This is because withdrawal from the heroin high leaves their skin insanely itchy. I could only wonder at what terrible things these children must have witnessed!

Somehow, we made it through that first visit experience. The days went by so fast it seemed we were always going through the cycle of the next visit. For the first few weeks, the parents were in rehab, so the transporter would pick up the kids, sit through their visit, then bring them home. One day the transporter complained to me how difficult it was to both drive and manage the children for the entire two-hour trip. Would I consider accompanying them?

I consented, thinking this would help create some stability of caretakers for the children. Tim agreed that it might even help us earn the trust of their birth parents. Tim, in turn, looked forward to getting some one-on-one time with our own kids, who desperately needed some personal time with their daddy.

I remember feeling nervous about walking into a drug rehabilitation center and meeting T-Man's and Kay-Kay's birth parents. Would they hate me? Would they even talk to me? I could not imagine what they must be experiencing. Not only had they lost their children but their dignity, confined as they were to a treatment center with strict rules and regulations.

The drug center had a nice family area for visitation. Seating myself on a chair in one corner, I watched a security guard lead T-Man's and Kay-Kay's birth mother into the visitation area. The children's mother was a beautiful woman with long, wavy hair, but years of drug abuse had taken a toll on her teeth, and the slow way she walked indicated frailty. She seemed passive and timid, sadness the only emotion in her eyes.

She immediately embraced both children. I quickly noticed that T-Man was showing more attachment and concern for her than his sister. He would brush at her hair with his "good" hand and look into her eyes, asking her if she was feeling okay.

In contrast, Kay-Kay was in perpetual motion, moving from toy to toy and bouncing all over her mother's lap. The visit sped by. Right before it was time for T-Man and Kay-Kay to leave, their mother reached into her pocket to pull out two coloring book pages.

"I made these for you," she told them. She had colored the pages beautifully, writing one of their names on each with a few words saying how much she loved them. This touched my heart. I knew she had nothing else to give them in that moment. Later when we were back at home, we taped each child's picture above their bed, and both T-Man and Kay-Kay would constantly reference them with love.

> *A Tip for Foster Parents: Regardless of how we feel about a birth parents' gifts, it is vital to both allow and encourage our foster children to enjoy and display their gifts as a visual reminder that their birth parents do love them.*

T-Man and Kay-Kay would receive gifts from time to time from their birth parents that were not so innocent or even age-appropriate (video games and movies were especially an issue), not to mention extravagance beyond what we could or would ever give our own kids. I've heard similar complaints from other foster parents about an absent, neglectful birth parent compensating by showering gifts as though to buy affection or even possibly to undermine the foster parents. But however much a foster parent might disapprove of a particular gift from the birth parents, I came to understand how vital it is to allow our foster children to enjoy and display their gifts (so long as they are age-appropriate) as a visual reminder that their birth parents do love them. We must lay aside any misgivings or even jealousy on our own part to embrace a birth parent's efforts, even if it is not what we would give our own birth kids.

At the end of that first visit, Kay-Kay suddenly remembered me. Dismissing her birth mother with a quick hug, she came bouncing over to me, shouting, "Let's go, *Mommy!*"

Their birth mom immediately turned her head to see who on earth her child was calling Mommy. It was the first time she'd noticed me, and I could feel her sizing me up and down. I was hopeful I'd passed her test, but I also saw bitter sadness and pain in her glance. No words were spoken between us.

The atmosphere was so different when we visited the birth dad, I chose not to enter the visitation area this time because the transporter had informed me the dad had an explosive temper and might become enraged by my presence. But I could hear T-Man and Kay-Kay laughing inside the room, and the transporter later told me their dad was chasing them around the room and tickling them. He'd also brought them gifts: candy — from the candy machine in the waiting room.

When the visit was over, the birth dad demanded to meet me. The transporter's introduction was rather hesitant, and my own hands were trembling as I shook his hand. His gaze was direct as he looked down at me to say with unmistakable sincerity, "Thank you for taking care of my children. I see they are in a good home. They look good, and I am very thankful you are the one taking care of them."

I was both shocked and pleased. Maybe this guy wasn't so bad after all! He seemed much older than the birth mom. Like her, he displayed a thin body and damaged teeth due to drug abuse, but the expression in his eyes was lively, and he walked with confidence.

After that, the agency asked if I would continue supervising all visits to the birth mom. Over the next two years, she showed great progress, going from the drug rehab center to a half-way house, which involves some monitoring but also encourages addicts to find a job and learn to live independently. Once she completed the half-way program, she moved in with a boyfriend. Though she did struggle with stability in relationships, she was at least making progress at remaining clean and bonding with her children.

Since she still had no car of her own, I would drive T-Man and Kay-Kay to a MacDonald's within walking distance of her current home, and the agency would reimburse me for my fuel. I would also fill out reports on the visits, whether she actually showed up for them, her reactions to the kids, after-effects of the visits, etc. Not that these reports really mattered. So long as the birth mother made the slightest effort to participate in at least one visit every six months, the court system did not require any kind of update as to how the visits were actually going.

I never took my own children to these visits. Our foster kids became quite different children during these visits, and I did not want my birth children exposed to the confusion of the visits. It felt strange to have a child calling out "Mommy!" to two starkly different women. Besides, I wanted to give my birth children some alone time with their own daddy or grandparents.

During the visit, I would always sit some distance away,

occupying myself on my phone. If the children came over to me, I would shoo them back to their mom. In time, their birth mom and I grew close, though she only made it to about half her scheduled visits. Sometimes she would cancel while we were making the one-hour drive because she hadn't woken up in time or something had "come up". But at least she was trying and communicating with me.

Occasionally we would drive all the way to the McDonalds, only for her not to show at all. It pained me to explain those occasions to T-Man and Kay-Kay. They knew exactly why we were waiting, and even though I tried to make excuses for her, they knew their mommy had failed them.

Their birth father was another story. I did not feel comfortable being around his short-tempered personality, and even the transporter struggled with his attitude. So I never supervised any of those visits. He never made it past his initial rehab. He got mad at the rehab center personnel and ended up escaping to the streets. After that I'd assumed he'd be out of our lives permanently. Two years went by without him making it to a single visit. Nor did he ever call or show any interest in pursuing a relationship with his children.

Visits typically landed on a Friday, so we dubbed Fridays our family party day, most commonly pizza and a movie. We wouldn't start the pizza and movie until all the children were safely home. This meant Tim and our birth kids would be waiting for however long it took for me to return with T-Man and Kay-Kay after a visit. We would then rent a movie, order in pizza, and all stay up late. It was such a fun way to end a terrible day.

We always invited the social workers to join us if they happened to show up during our parties. Who could refuse a hot, delicious pizza? Once we even had a surprise visit from the children's guardian-at-large (GAL), the attorney appointed to represent our foster children in court. She enjoyed our movie and pizza along with us, and it made a lasting impression of kindness.

Our open-door policy remains to this day, and our celebrative Fridays are still a fantastic way to end any week. Even years later with no foster children in our home, we still celebrate Movie and Pizza Night on Fridays.

> *A Tip for Foster Parents: Take every opportunity to participate in your foster kids' visits with their birth parents.*

I cannot recommend strongly enough for foster parents to participate in supervising their foster kids' visits. It provides a terrific opportunity for any foster parent to become more involved in their foster children's lives. I am so thankful I agreed to do so. I was able to see firsthand what the kids were experiencing during their visits instead of relying on a transporter who might or might not tell me what happened.

I also discovered I was wrong to ever fear the birth parents. I was now making every effort to get to know them. After all, my foster children came from these people. I wanted to be able to tell them stories about their family background as they grew up. After all, we all love to hear stories about our beginnings and family history, whether good or bad. I did ask the birth mom for her children's baby pictures, and she gave me all she had. And I took as many new pictures as I could, which I put in colorful scrapbooks for T-Man and Kay-Kay to look back on in future years.

I made photo albums for their birth mom with current pictures of T-Man and Kay-Kay. I always remembered her birthday, Mother's Day, and Christmas, making her some small gift in hopes of brightening her day a little. I did the same for the birth father and would give the photo albums to the agency, which I hoped would be passed on to him.

One promise Tim and I made together was to never, ever say anything negative about the foster children's biological family in their presence. Only behind the closed door of our bedroom would I blow off steam to my husband after a particularly terrible visit. Communicating my own frustrations about the birth parents to my spouse was important to me, but I tried my best not to do so in front of any of the kids.

I do believe that if we truly love our foster children, we must also love the parents from whose DNA those children were formed. Scripture has strong words about claiming to love God but not others:

> "A new command I give you: Love one another. As I have loved you, so you must love one another. By this everyone will know that you are my disciples, if you love one another."
> (John 13:34-35)

Similarly, to say, "I love my foster kids but hate their parents," minimizes the truth that those foster kids are, in fact, the offspring of those parents. To reject their parents is to reject the children. Sometimes our foster kids' parents would demonstrate behavior and habits so frustrating I might have felt entitled to dislike them. I can certainly admit to failing many times in my efforts to love them. But Tim and I both tried hard to value the parents who had given birth to these children we loved. After all, their birth parents had chosen life for these kids, an amazing feat in itself in today's world of choice when abortion would have been such an easy alternative.

Love is a difficult task. And despite my efforts, sometimes my anger would clash with my love. For instance, once the mother began making significant progress, the court increased her visitation hours. She was now permitted unsupervised visits up to three hours once a week. No longer would I be present to protect the kids.

At this time, she depended on her current boyfriend for transportation, so I would drive the kids to a half-way point where the mom and boyfriend would pick them up. After one such visit, T-Man told me about an incident with an older half-brother, his mom's son from a different father. Four years older than T-Man, this boy was in the custody of another family member, but would join his mom and younger siblings during these unsupervised visits. What T-man described to me was a situation of improper boundaries between the step-siblings while his mother was watching TV in another room. I had no choice but to report it to the Mandated Reporter Hotline.

There was an investigation, but unfortunately, nothing came of it, and the visits continued as before. How do you balance the anger you feel with the love you are supposed to feel for an inattentive parent who continues to neglect their children? I expressed my frustrations with her poor parenting abilities in my journal and late at night in my husband's arms.

Visits are one of the hardest parts of being a foster parent. It is beyond description on how difficult it is to give up your kids and see them crumble back into the old behavior patterns you have fought so hard to rid from their lives. Visits remind you that these children are not yours. They belong to a system that seems to go on and on and on. And when those visits become overnight visits, you can expect the children to be impacted even more profoundly, resulting in major demonstrations of regression.

I praise God that our foster children's overnight visits included a total of only four weekends during our entire three-year journey of fostering. This is where I believe God answered my many prayers and crying out to him over these visits because God did rescue us from years of overnight visits. He did deliver us from countless unsupervised hours with parents who were not really ready to protect and care for their own.

God did not stop all visits from happening. But he was faithful to our petitions and to his promises in his Word. God foresaw the future and knew that these children needed to be somewhat bonded to their parents. Every time they did have a visit, God was there, protecting and delivering our foster children from who knows what kind of harm might have happened.

I don't want the discouraging realities of the visits I've just described to sway anyone who might be reading this from the great blessing fostering can be. In truth, while our foster children might be gone a few hours a week, the remainder of the time they were safely in our home. I had the constant joy of being their number one provider and nurturer. Tim would remind me of how much they had progressed since coming to our home.

"Of all the ministries we have tackled together, fostering is by far the most rewarding," he would say repeatedly. "There is nothing that can compare to watching a child bloom right in front of your very eyes, just by giving him a chance for success."

The many hugs and kisses we received once T-Man and Kay-Kay returned home after a visit quickly erased those feelings of separation and anxiety. I would constantly remind myself that even though the children were gone for the next few hours, they were in my home for many, many hours. Any pain involved in a few hours of separation and worry was far outweighed by the blessings of having them in my home most of the time.

From the Voice of Experience:

"The first ten months our foster daughters were with us, the mention of going to visit their biological mom resulted in squeals of joy. That was great for them. But for me, that left me feeling sub-par. I woke at the break of dawn with them. I tended all their boo-boos and upset tummies. This other woman, their birth mom, gets to put on her happy face for two or three hours a week and just play with them. She gets to show off the best, put-together self she has. And I am left with all the hard work of raising her toddlers. It hurt. Last month, though, something changed. The mention of going to visit their birth mom now brought cries of "No! I don't want to! I want to stay here with you!" All the hard work of mine to bond to them has finally paid off. They feel the love I have for them. But as I pry their precious little arms off my neck to put them in their car seats to head out for their visit, I feel sick. This actually hurts much more than those first initial joyful squeals. This is now painful for them while I rejoice. I don't want to see them hurting. Please, let me have back the pain. I will hurt instead of them. Why did I ever think this would be better?"

—A. G., foster and adoptive parent.

7 DISCIPLINE

We don't get to wait to offer our lives until we have our acts together. We don't get that luxury. If we did, would anyone ever feel like offering anything? God asks us to be vulnerable. He invites us to share and give in our weaknesses. He wants us to offer the beauty that He has given us even when we are keenly aware that it is not all that we wish it were. He wants us to trust Him. —from "Captivating" by John Eldredge

Sometimes, it seems a foster parent never gets to truly rest. If I wasn't juggling parental visits and doctor's appointments, I was at home trying to break apart fights and teach good morals. Disciplining a foster child can seem as unachievable as teaching an elephant to fly. Much like breaking a horse, it takes immense patience. You must focus on the goal and not the process of disciplining. You must never give up hoping for small glimpses of success.

When disciplining a foster child, the agency has strict rules. These include never physically hurting a child, never withholding food as punishment, and never placing a child in a closet or complete isolation. These rules are not hard to abide by, and they offer a peace of mind for all parties involved.

A more delicate area is balancing what may work for one child and what does not work for another child. In correcting my own children, a stern rebuke was typically all I needed. But I quickly discovered my own inadequacy in trying to get our foster children to respond to the same techniques. Yet unprepared and ill-equipped though I was, I committed myself to obey the task God had given me of raising four beautiful gifts from God. I knew that God could use even my weaknesses. That my vulnerability is beautiful in his eyes, opening me up to accept and obey whatever God may be telling me to do, despite my inexperience.

Tim and I decided that it was best to treat all our children as equally as possible. We did this with disciplining too. Whatever we did with the foster children, we did with our kids. We had to accommodate the foster agency's rules into our family and become exceptionally creative. Here were some of the effective tools we used:

- **No dessert:** We never withheld nutritious food or a meal, but sweets are a privilege.
- **Running:** Examples include running laps around the house or to a tree and back.
- **Extra chores:** Chores could be taking out the trash or cleaning a room, but always age appropriate.
- **Time outs:** I tried to use these sparingly, since foster children do not respond well with being isolated. My time outs were always in an open room like the kitchen or living room and never for more than ten minutes.
- **Putting away toys:** Specifically any toys that provoked fighting. If we couldn't all play nicely, then those particular toys all went away.
- **No TV:** This didn't work for Kay-Kay who hated TV anyway but all the other children responded well.
- **Quiet time:** I loved this one. This was not quiet time in isolation. Everyone would continue doing what they were doing, but quietly. This would give everyone a chance to think and eliminate tension.
- **No outside time or other privileges:** This might include playdough, puzzles, or our nightly story-time reading.

I made my own tools for managing and teaching positive behavior. I used a good behavior award chart, trying to focus on rewarding positive behavior vs. punishing the negative. I tried to eliminate the everyday stresses that contribute to negative behavior by having the children complete five tasks a day to care for themselves. These tasks included eating breakfast, brushing their teeth, making their bed, getting dressed, and picking up their clothes. Once their tasks were completed, they could then "high-five" a picture of a palm I had made and placed in our living room.

For me, being fair and consistent was the trickiest part of disciplining. Our foster children demanded much more attention than my own birth children. I was thankful for the prior years I'd had with just my own kids as this made my job easier. I could trust my own kids to know my expectations and respond accordingly. I've come to understand that years of adult neglect and mistrust will take just as much time, if not more, to undo in a foster child's life if they are to learn how to function within a healthy family, which requires rules, routines, stability and consistency.

Along the way, I've also come to understand that as parents we need to use caution in the way we confront our kids. Not just demanding their respect, even though there is justification for such demands, but instead requesting their obedience out of love for God and for each other. We as parents must communicate always that God is good. He disciplines us because he is good. As parents, we model his goodness when we discipline our children. We ask our children to obey us. We ask them to enter into a relationship with us. Together, parents learn the art of disciplining, and children learn the rewards of obedience. This is a matter of trust.

Foster children need to know we want what is best for them. We must prove to our foster children that they can trust us. And that discipline is an effective way to love. In fact, if we go back to the very beginning of the human race, we can see God as the perfect Father displaying for us just how to discipline.

Setting Clear Consequences

When we read the story of Adam and Eve (Genesis 2-3), we can see that they viewed God as more than just a Creator. He was their friend and father. They were in constant relationship with him. God gave them clear and defined expectations when he told them not to partake of the Tree of the Knowledge of Good and Evil or they would die.

However I try I fail so miserably in trying to communicate my expectations to my children. Many times, I am not very clear on the punishment because I do not anticipate disobedience. I desperately want to believe they won't need a punishment. I hope for the best and believe they won't want to disobey. When I do anticipate disobedience, I usually end up giving meaningless consequences with poor follow-through. For example: "Don't touch the vase, or I will put you in time out."

I have learned that with foster kids, you must be careful not give them the idea of disobedience. By making such a statement, I am planting the seed of them disobeying just to earn my attention. Especially since "time-out" can become quite the game with a foster kid. One, it singles out the child and lets them get my emotions all riled up making that child the center of my world. Two, Kay-Kay especially excelled at screaming her head off, picking her nose until it bled, or some other response that would force me to come and relieve her from time-out.

Finding the balance of a perfect punishment with a flawless follow-through has been a struggle. I've learned to bounce the ideas of reprimands with my husband. He helped me brainstorm one such idea of making colorful poster boards so all the children could see. Though in reality, the poster boards were so *I* could be reminded of the consequences. Here are just a few of the reminders and their consequences we wrote up on posters:

- WE RESPECT OTHERS.
- YOU SPILL IT, YOU CLEAN IT.
- YOU OPEN IT, YOU CLOSE IT.
- YOU HIT, YOU SAY YOU'RE SORRY.
- YOU LIE, FIX IT BY TELLING THE TRUTH.
- IT'S NOT YOURS! ASK FIRST BEFORE YOU TAKE IT.
- YOU TURN IT ON, TURN IT OFF.
- YOU LEAVE THE TOILET SEAT HOW YOU WANT TO FIND IT
- YOU LOVE, YOU RESPECT.

This also took the pressure off me as the bad guy. If one of the rules wasn't being followed, we could just refer to the corresponding poster and be creative together on a fair consequence. The goal became to help the offender remember and in the future choose to respect others. It became a very matter-fact, cause-and-effect response to a disobedience instead of a heated battle. And let me tell you, a foster child loves a heated battle!

God also taught me some ideas on how to discipline through studying how he handled his own children's first sin.

Having Consistent Follow-Through

When Adam and Eve sinned, one would think God would get angry and start yelling. As a parent, I would be shouting: "How many times have I told you not to . . .? Why didn't you listen to me? As soon as I turn my back, you disobey? What's wrong with you? I am just so upset with you right now! How can I ever trust you? Do you hate me? I wish that for just once you would . . ."

As an imperfect parent loaded with sin, my tendency is to accuse and belittle. My anger rises quickly inside of me. I get annoyed. I have to stop whatever important business I'm doing to focus my all attention on a situation I didn't plan for. I get frustrated with the children's lack of desire to please me. I get tired. I give up easily. I yell, and then I feel guilty. Sometimes it feels like I'm on some crazy carnival ride, a dark, depressing Ferris wheel that's going 'round and 'round endlessly, never letting me escape the dizzying cycle of my own inadequacies.

I have a terrible time with follow-through. Especially if my child starts to cry, beg, or bargain with me. I'm a huge push-over, which makes a terrible parent. I get played more than I am willing to admit. And our foster children, who had broad experience in manipulation, got away with even more. I will tell you this story as an illustration.

One day while we were visiting at my sister's house, Kay-Kay was playing by a broken window. I had told her not to touch it and to go play somewhere else. When I wasn't looking, Kay-Kay made her way back to the window. My mom was watching and told her, "No. Don't touch that."

Kay-Kay let out a blood-curdling scream. She then started crying and wailing, "She hurt me! She hurt me!"

Running into the room, I snatched Kay-Kay up into my arms. Wrapping her own arms around me, she glared at my mom. Turning to my mom, I demanded accusingly, "What happened? What did you do?"

"Nothing," my mom responded calmly. "I just told her not to touch the window."

I didn't know who to believe, my mother with whom I'd lived my entire life or a screaming, tearful preschooler. It took me a long time to figure out that I had a very manipulative child in our home. My mother had never touched Kay-Kay.

Unfortunately, Kay-Kay received no punishment for her

disobedience over the window. I would find myself manipulated by her time and time again, which in turn would make me feel irritated. I would lash out in frustration, then feel guilty about my quick explosion.

Giving a Chance for Repentance

If only I could address my children's misbehavior as perfectly as God addressed his children's first sin in the Garden of Eden (Genesis 3:8-13). First, God doesn't rush in with fierceness or anger, but walks calmly to meet Adam and Eve, even though he knows full well what they have done. If I knew in advance of my child's sin, believe me, I would not be strolling in to meet with them.

God's calmness doesn't keep Adam and Eve from feeling so guilty that they hide from him. In response, God asks them three questions to which he already knows the answers but still takes time to ask: "Where are you? Who told you that you were naked? What is this you have done?"

Our all-knowing God not only asks for a response from his misbehaving creation but waits for their response, something else I fail at. I get so caught up in my child's disobedience, that I whip out a million reactions and questions; my sinning child never gets a chance to say one word. If my child does muster the courage to butt in, my annoyance is even further magnified when they don't respond exactly as I expect. My children have learned fast just to say nothing.

In contrast, God calmly asks a question, then waits for his children to process and think things through. I think he is also waiting for a repentant heart. Unfortunately, though God gives both Adam and Eve the opportunity to respond, we don't see Adam, Eve, nor the snake uttering a single word of repentance in the Genesis 3 account.

As parents, we need to give children a chance to process their actions. They need to have room enough to respond without fear of Mommy's reaction. God's patience in this story is a beautiful picture of his divine character. Once Adam and Eve finally do respond, God matter-of-factly restates the consequences of their sin. It's a big blow with painful consequences. This included separation from God, eventual physical death, and spiritual death. I can't imagine how hard this must have been for God as a loving parent to carry out the consequences to their decision to sin. But God follows through with the punishment that he said would occur.

Effective Tools of Discipline Require a Relationship

It took me a long time for figure out a discipline plan that could work with a highly devious child. Only through a loving and intimate relationship can one even have the patience to pursue a plan. With Kay-Kay, I confess I never did find a single, well-defined discipline tool. Anything I tried would only work so often. Then I would have to be creative and switch it up or I'd get played again by her manipulation. Making her run laps around the house seemed to be the most efficient way for us both to have some time and space from each other to process. For me, it was time to calm down and think of a plan of action. For her, it provided a way to exhaust some of the energy that comes with the thrill of disobedience.

Of course children don't have to be in the foster system to be rebellious. We see this in the Parable of the Prodigal Son, (Luke 15:11-32), a story Jesus told of a father with two sons. The youngest son was a perfect example of a child who is always pushing and pulling and trying to get all the attention. This youngest son demands his inheritance right now, which in essence is telling his father he wishes he were dead.

In Jewish culture, this was so disrespectful a father could be expected to disown the son. Instead, the father gives into his son's demands, almost as though he is waiting to see if the son will back down and repent. But instead of repenting, the son goes off and wastes his entire inheritance. Only when he is stuck feeding pigs with no money or food does he think of his father.

It is at this point the son works up a manipulative scenario of how to win back a place in his father's home. He practices this speech: "I will say to my father, 'I have sinned against heaven and against you, but let me be like one of your hired workers.'"

The son knew that at his father's home he wouldn't have to fight pigs for scraps to survive. His father was not just a good dad but a good employer. So why go hungry when he could get ample food to eat just by becoming his father's servant? Notice that the son is still thinking only of himself. His entire speech of repentance is designed just to fill his empty belly and get treated better than he currently deserves.

But the story makes clear that the father wasn't waiting for a repentant heart. He didn't even wait for the son to make his speech. Instead, he ran to the ungrateful son, hugging and kissing him. Then he threw his son a huge barbecue party, treating him like royalty.

Our actions speak louder than our words. I couldn't count the times I've demanded of our kids, "Say you're sorry NOW!" Don't get me wrong. We all know children need to be taught how to say they are sorry. But the best way they learn is from our actions.

Leading the Way by Modeling Repentance

God convicted me strongly that if I want my children to

display repentance, my own life needs to be a living witness. So if Tim and I argue in front of the kids, we also apologize in front of the kids. If I lose my cool with the children, I will also bow my head, praying out loud for forgiveness, then turn around and apologize to them for losing my temper. Demanding that children say they are sorry really doesn't work if we never model it for them. Modeling what we want from a child is far more effective than strong persuasion. Otherwise, our children can easily become resentful.

As Jesus continues to tell this story, we see the older son become resentful, (Luke 15:25-32). His younger loser of a brother comes back from wasting his inheritance, and instead of punishment, his dad throws him a party?!

Angry, the older son refuses to attend the party. This is where the father illustrates true humility and what it means to be a leader and unifier of his family. Instead of indignantly demanding obedience, he goes out to where his disgruntled older son is and begs him to join the family celebration. He doesn't belittle the validity of his older son's feelings, but affirms that he has always been a responsible and hard-working son. He also makes clear there are still consequences for the younger son's bad behavior, who has now lost his inheritance.

"You have always been a good son," the father sums up [author's paraphrase]. "And all I have is yours. But now it's time to celebrate that your brother is alive. Now come on, let's go love on him!"

A Parent's Job to Constantly and Consistently Unite the Family in Love

As parents, we are the unifiers of the family. It is up to us to encourage our children to be friends. Yes, competition is fierce. It may be easy to label the foster children as "bad" and the birth children as "good". After all, we tend to be a little biased towards our own flesh and blood.

I acknowledge that at times I became so focused on trying to correct negative behavior in our foster children that my own children were not rewarded or complimented on their good behavior. They were constantly watching our parenting, and it would be easy for bitterness to set root in their hearts even at such early ages. It was up to us parents to be the leaders in fostering love and unity among our children.

My husband and I pray daily for our parenting and for our children to love each other. Every night when my kids go to sleep and every morning when my kids leave for school, I pray this simple but meaningful prayer: "Lord, may they love you with all their heart, soul, strength and mind, and love their brother and sister as themselves."

I don't expect this to come naturally. I don't just dream of my children being all buddy-lovey without me first encouraging the initiative. The good father in this story did exactly that. He didn't want either one of his sons to leave. He wanted them both together, both celebrating. He didn't favor either. He was the unifier of the family.

To Discipline Is to Love

True parental discipline should always be out of love. God gives us the greatest example of loving discipline. The author of the New Testament book of Hebrews reminds us:

> "My son, do not make light of the Lord's discipline, and do not lose heart when he rebukes you, because the Lord disciplines the one he loves, and he chastens everyone he accepts as his son." (Hebrews 12:5-6)

My dad is a real-life example of a great discipliner. When we were disobedient, he would call my sisters and me into our room and talk to us. He would tell us he did not want to punish us and how much it hurt him to have to do so. But obedience to God meant loving us through discipline. He seldom yelled or got angry. After punishing us, he would leave us to think about our situation. After a few minutes, he always returned to hug us and assure us that no matter what we did, we could never stop him from loving us.

I have often heard people demand when something goes wrong, especially when something unexpected happens to them personally, "Why do bad things happen to good people?" Whether intentionally or not, they are implying that they are good, therefore undeserving of bad circumstances.

Not that all bad circumstances are God disciplining us. Sometimes we face trials to test us and our walk with God (James 1:2-4). Sometimes bad things are just the consequences of living in a sinful world. But sometimes God does discipline his children in order to purify us and correct us when we most need it.

I imagine it must be really hard to discipline me. I am pretty stubborn. When Tim asked for my hand in marriage, my father quietly reminded my future husband of my strong-willed spirit: "You do know she is a handful."

Tim cleverly responded, "I view her as a wild horse. You just need to learn how to channel that energy."

Yet it is this very streak of stubbornness that makes me able to accomplish hard things for God. Fostering is not for someone who won't fight. You have to really want to make a difference in someone's life and be willing to risk it all even being misunderstood and willing to not please everyone as you go along the journey.

Modeling Transparency to our Children

God uses our weaknesses for his glory, our imperfections for his causes. We need to be transparent with our children about our own weaknesses, modeling for them how God can one day also use their weaknesses for his glory. In Genesis 3, God uses Adam and Eve's weaknesses to present to us his perfect solution for their sin problem—Jesus—when he addresses the following to the serpent, who is Satan in animal form:

> "And I will put enmity between you and the woman, and between your offspring and hers; he will crush your head, and you will strike his heel." (Genesis 3:15)

Adam and Eve would still have to suffer the consequences of their sin, separation from God and ultimate physical death. But in this prophecy, God is giving them the promise that one of their descendants would crush the head of the Serpent who had deceived them, even though Satan would fight back and strike his heel.

That promise was fulfilled in the coming of the Messiah, God's own son, Jesus Christ, whom Satan indeed attempted to strike down by instigating his crucifixion. Instead, through his willing sacrifice on the cross, Jesus destroyed once and for all the works of Satan. And just as God sent his Son to pay the penalty for our sins so that we might receive forgiveness, forgiveness becomes for us the greatest example we can model for our own children.

Keeping No Record of Wrongs

After disciplining, we must also be willing to forgive and move on. Forgive and forget. My dad modeled this to his children, and he remains my hero to this day. I know that he loves me and that I can never do anything to stop him from loving me. I want to be like my father and the good father from the Parable of the Prodigal Son, waiting patiently for my children to know without a doubt that nothing they can do will quench my love for them. My love is not based on their actions, whether good or bad. My love cannot be manipulated. I will always love them whether they stand beside me or run from me. This is the inheritance I must pass on to my kids.

From the Voice of Experience:

"If I could speak to the foster boy that I was years ago and tell him one thing, I would ask him to do a better job of listening and doing what is expected the first time asked and not waiting to obey only on the fifth time asked. I'd tell him that he has been given an amazing gift of a loving family who took him into their home, and yet he still tries to give them grief. Looking back now as a man on my childhood, my behavior was totally unacceptable.

I would like to tell my foster dad, who passed away when I was fifteen years old, that I am sorry for the grief I caused. I believe my foster family didn't view my misbehavior as grief, but understood that I was a young child from a broken home and that their efforts of trying to mend those broken pieces has made me into the amazing individual that I am today. It just took a bunch of bumps and bruises to mold me. You cannot hold foster children's past life against them and bring it up. Otherwise, it is like giving them a crutch to fall back onto if things don't go right."

—A.H., a former foster child who is now a seventh-grade math teacher, volleyball and track coach, spouse, and father of three.

8 REACTIVE ATTACHMENT DISORDER

It has been said: time heals all wounds. I do not agree. The wounds remain. In time, the mind, protecting its sanity, covers them with scar tissue and the pain lessens, but it's never gone.
—Rose Kennedy

My journal entry:

> *She brings out all the ugly in me. Proved to me that I need Jesus all the more! She snuggled me. I thought, Aw! A sweet moment. Then I felt her dig her chin into my breast. Ouch, I thought in my head, but bit my tongue and smiled. Nope. I'm not gonna let her know it hurts! I even snuggled her all the more! She loves me - she loves me not! Crying, screaming, shouting. Does she need to express herself this way? Ok. Go ahead. I need to give her crazy answers for crazy, attention seeking questions. These are fun and make everyone laugh. "Yes, I eat pinecones because they grow pine trees in my tummy and tickle me inside-out." I'm becoming more creative. This is good for me. Maybe it's just best to know that "joy comes in the morning" (Psalm 30:5). Erase this day. Delete. Do-over tomorrow. It's easy to love someone when they love you back. But it takes God-love to love someone who rejects your every intention. Choosing the narrow road is lonely—but godly.*

It didn't take me long to notice something oddly emotionally wrong with Kay-Kay. Despite his physical disabilities, her brother seemed "normal" in comparison. Sure, T-Man had Cerebral Palsy and limped. He needed physical therapy and speech therapy. He needed dental surgery. But his emotional health was good. The more he was around us, the fewer tantrums he displayed. He was not defiant but kind, obedient, and affectionate. He loved pleasing authority and earning rewards. He was truly bonded with us *and* his birth parents. His scars of the past were only physical. Those can heal.

Emotional scars are hidden and harder to detect, which makes healing from those wounds more difficult. Kay-Kay was physically perfect. She was beautiful and had energy for two people. She could be funny, charming and loved attention. But something about her behavior instinctively concerned me. I eventually discovered that Kay-Kay struggled with Reactive Attachment Disorder (RAD), a disorder I knew nothing about before fostering and that would keep me on my knees in prayer.

It is important to discuss this topic because it is typical in foster children because of the attachment issues that they have encountered. My intention is not to discourage anyone from fostering, but provide information that will help you understand and be able to anticipate this should it happen. And RAD can be frightening. One out of four foster children could show signs of RAD, so it is imperative for would-be foster or adoptive parents to understand what living with a child with this disorder looks like.

Lack of Love and Attachment Becomes Pattern of Pain

Every day it seemed we were bonding closer and closer with T-Man. I saw the opposite with Kay-Kay. She appeared to bond immediately with us as a family upon arrival, disparaging her former caregivers and smothering me with affection. But as time progressed, that affection became doled out as forms of manipulation or to make my other children jealous. Her displays of love frequently turned out to have some twisted purpose.

For example, when I put her to bed at night, she would say sweetly that she had a secret for me. When I leaned close to hear it, she would whisper slowly, "I love . . . Mommy X [her birth mom]!"

At first, I was all teared up since any average person would be expecting her to say: "I love you!" She would even stretch out the break between "love" and "Mommy" for a delayed reaction. Mastering my own disappointment, I assured Kay-Kay it is always good to love, especially her mommy. But inside my heart, I was concerned. How could a child just turning four years old know so well how to manipulate my emotions? Strangely, she knew I wanted her love and used that as a ploy to cause me pain.

Obsessively Lying

Kay-Kay's lies weren't out of need. Nor even to escape punishment as would be quite normal for children. She lied just to provoke a reaction. Seemingly stupid lies. Lies she knew would quickly create a disruptive scene in our home. An example would be the day I discovered her with chocolate all over her face and hands.

"Did you get into the chocolate in the pantry?" I asked her calmly.

Eyes wide and expression sincere, she responded, "No."

"But you have chocolate all over you," I continued.

"No, I don't!" she contradicted.

This could go on and on. There was no point to even trying to prove her wrong. It might seem laughable, but after twenty such lies a day, it wore me out emotionally. I also had to struggle with trying to ignore her lying while teaching the other children not to lie.

I finally began responding to her lies matter-of-factly: "Kay-Kay chooses to crazy-lie again today!"

The other children would do the same when she lied to

them. A refusal to react to her lies usually made her find another "game" to play. We tried not to set her up with an opportunity to lie. So instead of prying for a confession with a question, we would just make a blank statement. For example, "I know you did eat the chocolate. So since you've already had your dessert, you won't be able to have any at supper time."

It took careful planning and much self-control not to fall into the trap of battling about her lying.

Compulsive Behavior with a Tendency to Constantly Get Hurt

It may sound like an exaggeration, but we were continuously battling "wounds" or "owies". One major factor was Kay-Kay's impulsiveness, which lacked any awareness of danger. My normal motherly response was to put Band-Aids on her scrapes and bruises, but that just seemed to fan the fire. She constantly picked at her wounds to the extent that her sheets always had blood on them.

I was in constant confusion on what to do. Should I bring attention to the problem or just ignore it? Ignoring only goes so far. And calling her out on it clearly gave her great satisfaction. But when blood began staining our cream-colored carpets or an outfit we'd just bought for her, I could ignore it no more.

I finally discovered one useful tool: Liquid Band-Aid. Brushed on like a clear nail-polish, this makes it hard for a child to reopen a wound. But though it is virtually pain-free, many times it wasn't worth the screaming fit Kay-Kay would throw if I put it on even the smallest cut. She could turn any accident event into a moment for drama where all the attention would go to her.

RAD children get a thrill out of creating chaos. It's almost as if their brain receives a "high" from all the negative, emotionally charged situations. Why? Because chaos feels normal for them. Their formative years of development were very chaotic, so an orderly, regulated routine feels limiting. We had "rescued" a child from a disruptive, neglectful home. But that didn't mean she would automatically love us or be thankful for a normal home. To the contrary, our stability caused her great discomfort.

However, at the same time, if there was any change of the normal routine, Kay-Kay would be the first to remind us. If we decided she should sit in a different chair or that this Tuesday we wouldn't make tacos, she would become upset to the point of a meltdown. She desperately needed structure even though she was the very one who would try to knock down any structure we put in place. It took excessive energy and purposeful intention not to be pulled into her chaos.

Insisting the World Revolve Around Them

If Kay-Kay wasn't the center of attention, she found a way to become the center of attention through misbehavior. She had a deep need for affection and care, and getting attention made her feel secure. But that attention had to include a strong emotional response from the caregiver, and since negative emotions are stronger than positive, yelling at her was a more satisfactory response than a smile and "good job!"

I remember one time she took off her skirt while at school. When I picked her up wearing only a short shirt and tights, she was downright gleeful at how distressed I was that everyone could see her underwear through the tights. The only way she got away with this was because she had a substitute teacher that day! I remember how she would deliberately put on an outfit backwards or inside out, hoping I would respond, "Come on, Kay-Kay, you know better!"

Of course, if I dared to make such a response, she would wail and scream, acting as though I had wounded her soul by asking her to change. Refusing to go to the bathroom before leaving the house or eat her meal were other areas where she could control and get attention. Even if I cooked her favorite meal, she might pretend she hated it just for the attention she received for fussing over her food or having to stay at the table after everyone else was done. The more negative that attention, the better!

We did come to understand at least somewhat why Kay-Kay would focus on meals for her misbehavior. To sit at a table and eat together is fellowship. And fellowshipping is an intimate, bonding experience. When our family eats together, we hold hands to pray. We shut off all distractions of TV or radio. We look into each other's eyes and talk.

A RAD child has often grown up with no schedule for eating. When they did eat, it would typically be in front of the TV or some other distraction that doesn't involve human interaction. So RAD children find the closeness of a family meal incredibly uncomfortable. Misbehaving to break up the harmony makes it more comfortable for them, if for no one else.

If that meal is a particularly enjoyable or a special event, a RAD child will deliberately try to ruin that moment. This can be displayed by refusing to eat, crying at the table, needing to go to the bathroom every two minutes, wanting something that is not on the table, or vomiting. Yes, vomiting will get everyone to stop in their tracks immediately! Kay-Kay would stuff her mouth without swallowing, then wait with wide eyes, hoping someone would notice. If someone dared to suggest, "Swallow before you choke!", she would make it her goal to either start choking or hold out even longer.

The only way we could get around this battling over food was to say something like, "The food tonight is not your favorite, Kay-Kay. You probably won't like it, so you'll just have to be hungry. I'm sorry, I know you probably won't eat tonight."

Which would then impel her to prove us wrong! It was best to have low expectations, so she could meet them every time.

Impulsivity that Imitates Hyperactivity

Kay-Kay's IEP (Individualized Education Program) included that she had to learn to control her impulses. This seemed a bit nitpicky to be on an IEP. After all, aren't all toddlers a bit impulsive? But after living with her for a while, we recognized that her behavior mimicked an attention disorder or hyperactivity. It was a perpetual motion of constantly changing, unproductive, illogical movements.

Such lack of control made her vulnerable to accidents and incredibly disruptive in the classroom. She couldn't sit with her classmates to sing a nursery song all the way through without jumping up to go do something else. It was also displayed by constant questions, chatter, and "Mommy, Mommy, Mommy!" so no one else could get a word in edgewise. It was attention-getting and became rapidly irritating such as the following monologue as she got dressed:

"Mommy, do you like this shirt? Do I put this hole through my head? Do I wear it backwards? Mommy, what about these armholes? I think I could put my feet in here. Are you watching, Mommy? I said, I might need to put my feet in here. Mommy, do you like purple? This is a purple shirt, right? You do like purple, don't you? Well, I like pink! Did you know pink is my favorite color? What if I don't wear a shirt?"

Of course she already knew exactly how to get dressed. But quietness is intimate, and being alone can be intimidating for the RAD child, so this was a way of self-coping and to break up the inner tension.

Lack of Empathy

At first, I thought Kay-Kay just hadn't had any proper example of good morals. But it went much deeper than that. Her brain lacked cause-and-effect thinking. In other words, recognizing what the effect on someone will be if you do something to hurt them—or *caring* what the effect will be!

Kay-Kay couldn't put into words just why she chose to lie or hurt someone. I would make her say she was sorry for actions like hitting as a training exercise to develop empathy. But this seemed ineffective. I kept hoping she would eventually develop compassion for others and understand the whys behind our expectations of good behavior and the rewards that come with it. In the end, only God can change a heart, so I continued to hope.

No Fear of Strangers

Kay-Kay was incredibly charming and delightful around strangers. Ironically, this was one of my biggest struggles. No matter how much I tried to teach her, she didn't seem to believe me when I told her strangers can be dangerous. She would beg people she didn't know to pick her up, go into a room alone with her, or try to sneak away with them. Could a small child purposefully watch to make sure I wasn't looking, then deliberately plan to sneak away into the arms of a stranger? How can a parent be the protector of a child who will not listen to the voice of caution?

Many days it felt I was going 'round and 'round in a crazy circle. No form of correction or discipline would work. No matter how I tried to connect with Kay-Kay, by the end of the day I felt manipulated and even farther from her. I began to believe I was a failure as a parent and needed counseling. I thought I was causing her even more damage. I decided it was a personality clash and she needed to be with someone else, anyone else but me.

My realization that it wasn't just me came when she went to PreK, then kindergarten. She would disobey the teacher on the simplest tasks like washing her hands, going to the bathroom, sitting for a story, coloring, and especially napping. Not to mention homework! Homework started in first grade. She would deliberately tear her pages or fill in the incorrect answers.

Of course, all children struggle with obeying authority. Obedience is not a natural tendency. But emotionally healthy children want to please people in authority, a caring, loving teacher in particular. But Kay-Kay had no interest in pleasing those in authority over her. I had no words, plan, nor advice for her teachers. The teachers were kind and patient with Kay-Kay. Together we vowed to pray for her. And now that I knew the battle was not with just me, I began to seek for answers.

From the Voice of Experience:

"I thought love was enough. I believed my warm home, nutritious food, structured rules, and unconditional love would be a gift that could heal any child. But if you have never experienced RAD, you really should not judge nor offer any advice. Sometimes the effects of RAD don't show up until puberty—and then the adoption is final. There are steps you can take to minimize the effects of RAD, but there is no cure. Sometimes love isn't enough. All you can do is take one day at a time and wish for the best and try to remember to start fresh each day with a new opportunity for hope or heartbreak."
—Anonymous

9 SEEKING SOLUTIONS

> *Reactive Attachment Disorder is defined as the condition in which individuals have difficulty forming lasting relationships. They do not allow people to be in control of them due to this trust issue. This damage is done by being abused or physically or emotionally separated from one primary caregiver during the first three years of life . . . If a child is not attached—does not form a loving bond with the mother—he does not develop an attachment to the rest of mankind. The unattached child literally does not have a stake in humanity.*—Magid & McKelvey, 1988

A Google search brought me across a fascinating website: www.attachment.org. No longer did I feel so alone. The website's author, Nancy L. Thomas, has written an insightful book I highly recommend to anyone working with children from broken homes: *When Love Is Not Enough: A Guide to Parenting Children with RAD*. The above quote I found on this website described my foster daughter as though the author knew her.

While many foster children will have RAD or a form of attachment disorder, you do not have to be a foster or adopted child to experience an attachment disorder. This disorder can occur when a parent does not respond to the needs, physical or emotional, of a child. For instance, a baby cries because they are wet or want to be held. If no one responds or comforts them, the baby learns not to rely on the caregiver for their needs.

Healthy babies don't want to be separated from their mother. They need love, and even before birth they have bonded with their mother. But a baby left to fend for herself becomes a survivor. At age three, Kay-Kay could cook Ramen Noodles, feed herself along with her five-year-old special needs brother, and protect T-Man. But such impressive survival skills are the result of abandonment. This abandonment creates a deep rage in the soul as psychologist and RAD pioneer John Bowlby verbalizes well:

> "There is an inability to love or feel guilty. There is no conscience. Their inability to enter into any relationship makes treatment or even education impossible." (The Making and Breaking of Affectional Bonds. Bowlby, 1979)

A drug addict is so focused on their next fix that a crying baby becomes an annoyance and burden. This annoyance in turn can be tuned out and made easier to manage with more drugs. A drug addict is a neglectful and abusive parent because of the fixation for more drugs. When I asked Kay-Kay's birth mom to tell me stories about her as a baby, she could not remember even one. How could that be? It was as though that time frame did not even exist for her.

During the hour visits I supervised, Kay-Kay's mom was affectionate with kisses and hugs for her children, even showering Kay-Kay with extra attention. But she could not handle the children on her own. They were only sixteen months apart, which meant she'd been balancing her drug addiction with two babies, including a toddler with severe birth defects, as well as a violent relationship with the children's father. Yet despite all she was facing, she chose life for her baby. Praise be to God! Kay-Kay was born premature but healthy.

I believe there would be fewer foster children if someone would just foster the parents. The birth parents usually have not known healthy parenting themselves. They continue an ongoing cycle of abuse and neglect. My heart is moved with compassion for both the parents and their children. But to break this cycle, there must be severe and immediate consequences. Our court system goes to extremes to avoid terminating the rights of birth parents, preferring to simply remove the child into a safe home and let the possibility of reunification be the motivator to prompt a parent to change.

That is where I entered the scene. In my naivety, I had believed providing love, warmth, education, nutritious food, and acceptance was enough. Now I know that it takes years of therapy, prayer, delicate patience, and kindness to build trust and undo the disaster of neglect. Even then, there may just not be enough time. I felt that Kay-Kay didn't really care if she had to leave and never see me again. She always seemed happy to go to a visit, but also happy when the visit ended. So long as she was the center of attention, she was bubbly and easy to get along with.

As I researched RAD and Attachment Disorders in general, I had many questions as to why this horrible condition occurs. Even in the same family, siblings can go through the same exact emotional or physical abuse, yet only one child turns out with RAD. Nor does the degree of abuse necessarily determine why a child might have this debility. Psychologists have not been able to determine why one child left in his crib for hours with pre-birth exposure to drugs might still not display a single sign of RAD while another child from an unwanted pregnancy or whose mother suffered post-partum depression might display full-blown RAD.

Attachment disorder can occur in any family if children are consistently unable to connect with their parents, especially between the ages of nine months and five years. Here is a list of events that can make a child develop RAD:

- An unwanted pregnancy.
- Post-Partum Depression.
- Fetal exposure to drugs, alcohol or trauma.
- Any form of abuse (sexual, physical, emotional).

- Neglect (65% of all foster situations are from some form of neglect, which means that a caregiver did not respond to a child's need for help, such as not feeding a child, not providing a safe and secure environment, not protecting a child).
- Separation from the caregiver, whether through divorce, death, foster care, or even hospitalization.
- Sickness such as ongoing ear infections, hernia, colic.
- Being in an environment with many different caregivers, aka, day care, orphanage, boarding school, shelters, etc.
- Emotionally distant or disapproving parents.

I tried to write off Kay-Kay's more disturbing behavior as a child just trying to cope. But as time progressed and we became more serious about adoption, I knew we needed to get help for her. There are various therapies for RAD children, some more recommended than others. But the purpose behind all of them is to create a bond of trust and attachment between the caregiver and child.

As a foster parent, such bonding techniques are not always useful for healing. After all, a foster home may just be a temporary home. How can I as a foster parent create an attachment, just to have my foster child torn away for a visit to the past with her birth mom? How can I assure her that she can trust me as her guardian and responsible authority when a social worker's decision might undermine everything I've accomplished with her? How can I bond with a child with RAD, only to be torn apart again by some courtroom official who has never even seen her face?

The cycle of mistrust seems inevitable. If I could get my social worker to approve Kay-Kay's need for therapy, this would label her as a special needs child. Which in turn becomes a financial aid check to the birth parents if they regain custody. I wanted the birth parents to *want* to be with their kids, not just want the kids because of a taxpayer-funded social security check.

I was still debating which was the best route to go and had just started filling out the paperwork for therapy when our case took a dramatic turn. For the past two years, we'd only had visits with their mom. If any of the birth parents regained custody, we assumed it would be her. She was doing well, maintaining contact, and even attending church. We began to have hope we could establish a life-long relationship with her and the kids.

Then without warning she suddenly stopped all contact. She began another relationship that affected her progress. She went back to the same behaviors that had caused her to lose custody. It was almost as if she sabotaged her success. She stopped communicating and just disappeared. Later we learned that she had gone to jail, which left us unsure of what the future would hold. Giving into despair, she slipped quietly from the case.

But by that time, the children's birth father had reappeared. He had missed two whole years of visitation and demonstrated little hope of change. With zero progress from the dad and the birth mom out of the picture, our hope of adoption now seemed possible. In April 2013, we signed the "intent to adopt" papers with the agency. My heart was soaring!

To speed up the adoption process, a personal lawyer friend advised us to petition the birth parents to let us become the children's legal guardians. This way the birth parents would still legally be their parents, and the children would not change their last name, but the children would stay with us indefinitely unless challenged by the birth parents on their own dime in court. Our social worker called a meeting with the birth parents, but only the dad showed up. We presented our best case to him:

"Termination of parental rights does not have to be the ultimate step. We can sign guardianship papers today, and you can still see the children. On our terms of course, but all this court stuff can end today."

Guardianship would remove the foster system from the case. The parents would no longer be regulated to meet their goals by the social agency. We would become the ones to make decisions for the kids. We could even travel. Meanwhile, the children could still see their parents. We gave our promise that our home would always be a welcoming place for the birth parents—if they were sober and clean.

That was when the birth dad leaned in to demand decisively, "You mean you don't want to foster them anymore? I thought you were like some form of a babysitter. You mean to tell me you want to keep my kids forever? Listen to me clearly! They are my flesh and blood. Over my dead body are you going to keep them!"

There was nothing more to be said. The birth dad made clear he wasn't going to budge. And for some inexplicable reason, that meeting was what motivated him to clean up his act. He stopped missing his visits with the kids. He got a job. He started being clean for all his drug tests. He was showing increased focus and determination like we had never seen for the past two years.

Even with the dad's sudden interest, I had hoped the caseworker would still petition for legal screening – which is the beginning step for the termination of rights based on the fact of his two-year absence. As our court date approached, I thought we still had a chance. In August 2013, the judge was ready to approve termination of parental rights. But before doing so, he asked our current caseworker, who was present at the proceedings, if the birth dad had done all he possibly could to prove he was a fit parent.

This was the moment we had been waiting for. Surely our caseworker, who had witnessed our love for the kids and the two-year absence of the father, would speak up on our behalf. We were stunned when instead the caseworker stood up and said, "Yes, your Honor, he has done all he can and continues to show progress. I believe he can regain custody of the children. He shows attachment to them, and I would like to ask the court to give him more time to prove he can do this."

The district attorney also advocated for the birth father, telling the judge that he'd dealt with the birth dad in other court cases and that in his opinion the birth dad could get his act together if the judge would just allow him six more months to demonstrate he was serious. Devastated and discouraged, I cried all the way home.

I didn't know how much longer we would have the foster kids. Even though the next court date was in six months, we could still be fostering them for years because at any moment one parent could regress while the other would need time to prove success. But I did recognize that asking for therapy to try to create a parental bond with Kay-Kay would be futile at this point, if not even more damaging. Somehow, we just needed to make it through these next six months together and see what would happen.

Over the following months, Kay-Kay's misbehavior intensified. By now I was used to it and tried my best just to let her have her bad days. If her behavior became a disturbance to everyone else, she was sent to her room where she was allowed to express herself in her way there. We insisted her door stay open, and she could always come out when she was ready. While some RAD children become violent, Kay-Kay did not display aggressive behavior as to be a danger to herself and others. She could contently play quietly in her room and often would end up just falling to sleep. It was her safety and comfort zone. And I never left her alone for more than a few minutes without checking on her.

I know personally how easy it is to think the worst about RAD children. I have seen countless news articles of disastrous adoptions where desperate parents try to "rehome" an adoptive child with RAD. While a sad situation, I can identify with how frustrating and hopeless it must feel to these adoptive parents. The constant demand for attention from a RAD child can exhaust all your efforts. Their demand for love feels like a bucket with a hole in it that can never be filled. Since they were not nurtured and taught how to have a loving relationship during a key stage of development, their behavior becomes a desperate effort to prove that they are loved.

I do believe RAD children respond better when placed in homes where they are the only child. But that luxury is not always available. And many times RAD is not diagnosed until the teen years. Or as with Kay-Kay, it might take many months of trying to understand the underlying cause of misbehavior. By which point it may be too late to reevaluate the placement so as to ensure the child is the only one in a home.

There is Hope: The Helen Keller Story

In case the above read as though I am trying to dissuade readers from fostering and/or adopting, let me add here some encouragement. The journey is exhausting but also hopeful. After all, some RAD children have become great pillars of their community. They are extreme survivors. They have an ability to overcome obstacles the rest of society can't even fathom.

Helen Keller is a perfect example of a RAD child turning their life around to become an inspiring figure of history. Helen Keller became deaf and blind at nineteen months due to complications from illness and a high fever, possibly scarlet fever or meningitis. With loss of hearing and sight, she'd also lost the normal ways parents and children communicate and bond, which in turn led to the loss of attachment with her parents. Helen showed many signs of a RAD child: stealing food, screaming, tantrums, hitting, eating like an animal. Teachers, nannies, family members, and others who witnessed her behavior came to see her as a monster with no hope for healing. They even suggested she be institutionalized.

But her parents refused to institutionalize her and didn't give up hope. They found a devoted teacher, Anne Sullivan, who took on the challenge of trying to teach Helen new behaviors. In time, Helen Keller learned how to read, write, even speak. But this took many, many years of devoted love and care. Until her own death forty-nine years later, Anne Sullivan remained Helen's constant companion and mentor.

That kind of dedication can break down the walls RAD children build around themselves. But I had three other children in our home. I just couldn't focus that much attention on one child to the neglect of the others.

Still, despite my frustration and inability to break through Kay-Kay's walls, I had great dreams and aspirations for her. I'd always encouraged Kay-Kay to channel her enormous energy into climbing, aerobics, dance classes, and swimming. She was an excellent swimmer and had the lung capacity to swim long distances under water. While her great determination mostly displayed itself in defiance, it also helped her outlast and outrun her peers in any P.E. activity. So I had dreams of her becoming an athlete who might inspire others.

Pick Your Battles

It was my mother who gave me the best advice on how to deal with Kay-Kay during this time period. I remained hopeful we could adopt Kay-Kay as our second daughter. But I couldn't wait until the adoption was final to address her misbehavior. By then it would be too hard to undo. A licensed counselor, my mother explained that the best way to reach a RAD child is through reverse psychology. So she suggested I needed to pick my battles. In other words, I should consciously choose not to engage in such "minor" battles as refusing to eat at the table or go to the bathroom, lying, deliberately doing homework wrong. Even such issues as picking at a wound and bleeding should be ignored if possible. The only battles I really needed to address were if Kay-Kay hurt someone else physically.

Make it a game, my mom also suggested. The game was for me, not Kay-Kay, to test how long I could go without letting anything she said or did get "under my skin". Conversely, I should "notice" any time Kay-Kay did something positive, then make a big deal about her good behavior. The hope, of course, being that in time Kay-Kay would learn to seek attention through good behavior instead of negative.

Since Kay-Kay's constant goal was to get a reaction from me, preferably negative, this was hard stuff! As a parent trying to raise a God-fearing young lady, I could pretend for a while, then Kay-Kay would throw me a curve ball. I would go for it and end up losing my temper. Leaving me with a desire to distance myself from her, so this became a constant balancing act for me.

Some days I tried to genuinely not care. Ironically, those days are now some of my best memories of Kay-Kay because we seemed to get along better on those days. But deep inside my heart, I knew I *did* care, and pretending not to care ate away at my soul. I wanted to bond with Kay-Kay. I wanted her to be a part of our family forever.

As we neared the three-year mark from when T-Man and Kay-Kay had first entered our home, I began earnestly praying, *God, how much longer?* I knew this constant struggle could not be healthy. Nor could I see how we could keep going with this lack of trust indefinitely.

From the Voice of Experience:

"It's probably true that 99% of all foster children have some type of attachment issue. Maybe it won't be full-blown RAD, but definitely expect a HARD child. I recommend waiting to become a foster parent until you have no other children in the home. It is only fair to the foster kids to give them as much attention, resources and time as possible. And it is only fair to other kids in the home that they do not have a new sibling that makes life miserable for the family. The potential harm a foster child could do to a birth child is just too great. There is a time for everything."
—Anonymous

10 UNSEEN BATTLE

Until you know that life is war, you cannot know what prayer is for.—John Piper

My ongoing struggle with Kay-Kay's RAD disorder brings me to the issue of spiritual warfare. Mainly because it didn't take me long to recognize that the problems we were dealing with from the time T-Man and Kay-Kay entered our home were not just physical and emotional, but a spiritual conflict involving unseen forces.

From my earliest childhood, I can remember my mother teaching my sisters and me to be sensitive to the spiritual world. In Bolivia where we grew up, people took evil seriously. Witchdoctors, or *curanderos* (healers), as they were also called, were admired, influential and feared. The rural community where we lived believed nothing could stand against their power.

Similarly, from the time we moved into this community, the witchdoctors sensed the Spirit of the Living God that indwelled us, which caused them in turn to fear us. Their fear led them to cast spells on our family, resulting in weird things happening around our home.

I remember one such time when I was about nine years old. We had been given a purebred Australian Shepherd puppy that was our family's pride and joy. She was so smart that we were training her to help us round up our horses and cattle. One night, my mother was awakened by a feeling of great urgency. Her spiritual unease was so overwhelming she felt sure that a witchdoctor was cursing our home at that very moment.

Bolting out of bed, she began praying God's protection over each of her children. She felt God's Spirit urge her to continue praying, so she went on pray God's protection over our physical home, our horses, our goats, pigs, even the fertile land that surrounded our home. Feeling peace at last, she went back to bed and slept soundly.

The next morning was Sunday so we all got ready and left for church. Right before leaving, my sisters and I patted and cuddled our precious bouncy, energetic puppy. But when we returned home from church, something felt wrong. As we approached our gate, no bouncing pup came to greet us.

Then we noticed something lying in the grass just right outside our fence. It was our adorable puppy. As we got close, we saw she was not only dead but already being consumed by worms. How could this be? We had just been gone for no more than a couple hours.

Hearing our screams, the neighbors came running. When they saw what had happened, they immediately concluded, "You have been cursed!"

At which point my mother was reminded of the urgency that had awakened her in the night. Sorrowfully, she told us, "I forgot to pray over the puppy!"

So what is more real, the seen and tangible or the unseen and nonphysical? Every single human being, whether they admit it or not, walks between two worlds: the physical world and the spiritual world. We are spiritual and physical beings. Every human is created in God's image. That image is just as much spiritual as it is physical. And just as we may face physical battles, so there is an unseen spiritual battle between good and evil going on around us at all times.

What we believe about the spiritual world is what makes us a good or bad soldier on that unseen battlefield. Christian author Catherine Marshall, wife of the well-known minister and chaplain of the United States Senate Peter Marshall, words this well in her novel Christy:

"Evil is real—and powerful. It has to be fought, not explained away, not fled. And God is against evil all the way. So each of us has to decide where we stand, how we're going to live our lives. We can try to persuade ourselves that evil doesn't exist; live for ourselves and wink at evil. We can say that it isn't so bad after all, maybe even try to call it fun by clothing it in silks and velvets. We can compromise with it, keep quiet about it, and say it's none of our business. Or we can work on God's side, listen for his orders on strategy against the evil, no matter how horrible it is, and know that he can transform it."

I live my daily life recognizing that everything is influenced by the invisible. That what we see in the physical world is a reflection of what is going on in the spiritual world. The apostle Paul in his first letter to the Corinthian church reminds us that as believers we need to focus on the unseen. The spiritual should be more real to us than the physical because its effects are eternal:

"So we fix our eyes not on what is seen, but on what is unseen, since what is seen is temporary, but what is unseen is eternal."
(2 Corinthians 4:18)

For Tim and me, this unseen spiritual battle seemed to increase drastically while we were serving in foster care ministry. Those who are lost are under Satan's control. They are his territory. As we minister to the lost and invite them into our homes, we are invading Satan's domain. He will fight back, and it will not be easy. Spiritual warfare is not just for pastors and veteran Christians. Every single person will encounter the devil and his army. But as believers, we must expect it, and we must be ready with a clear strategy and effective weapons, as the apostle Paul reminds us:

> "For though we live in the world, we do not wage war as the world does. The weapons we fight with are not the weapons of the world. On the contrary, they have divine power to demolish strongholds." (2 Corinthians 10:3-4)

What are our spiritual weapons? We are to put on the full armor of God (Ephesians 6:10-17) and carry the sword of the Spirit, which is God's Word (Ephesians 6:17; Hebrews 4:12). And with Christ, we have the advantage. I pray this section will make us all aware of the imperceptible and help us prepare for victory. After all, we are already more than conquerors in Christ Jesus (Romans 8:37). The battle is already won (John 16:33).

Four Levels of Intensity

In past chapters I have mentioned how our spiritual battle began even before our foster children entered our home. But once T-Man and Kay-Kay arrived into our home, the intensity of the battle increased. To simplify and categorize the spiritual warfare aspects of fostering, I will divide it into four levels of intensity from our experiences: the Visible, the Bondage of a Dysfunctional Court System, Spiritual Oppression via Our Own Weaknesses, and the Ultimate Battle of the Mind.

Intensity Level One: the Visible

The visible level is actually the easiest to fight. It is in-your-face, so you can't deny it. Since you can see it, you can react immediately to pray over it. This visible level is most obvious when something happens that is totally outside any normal circumstance. For example, we had lived in our current home for eight years without ever having seen a venomous snake anywhere around our property. We did have snakes, but never once had I seen a deadly one.

Then about a week after our foster children arrived, an unexpected event happened. Caleb and T-Man were outside playing while I was indoors preparing a meal. Bursting suddenly into the kitchen, Caleb announced excitedly, "Mommy, I just killed a snake!"

"Um-hum," I nonchalantly responded, continuing to peel the potatoes for our meal.

Caleb went on to describe details. "Yeah, we were playing, and T-Man almost stepped on a snake. I told him to stay away. Then I ran inside to get my BB gun. I pointed at the snake and shot. I hit him right in the eye, and he is dead."

Now Caleb had my full attention. This was no farfetched story from the mind of a creative five-year-old! Dropping what I was doing, I ran outside. To my disbelief, I saw a water moccasin lying dead in the grass. A pit viper like copperheads and rattlesnakes, the water moccasin is North America's only venomous water snake. And while they can be found in Illinois, I'd never seen one before, much less this close to our house, which sat a full hundred feet from our pond, the nearest body of water.

The remarkable elements of this story are two-fold. First, the unusual presence of this venomous snake in my backyard. Second, that my five-year-old son had managed to kill the snake by shooting a BB in its eye on his first shot. Recalling his story, I pictured how close my son had to be to shoot such a tiny target. What if the kids would have stepped on the snake? What if Caleb had missed and the snake turned on him?

A few weeks later, I decided to take the kids to a fishing park where we could have a picnic while the kids fished. My mom had volunteered to help me with the kids, but since she wasn't ready, I suggested she meet us there. When we arrived at the park, I helped the kids set their hooks, then settled them along a lake bank to fish while I spread our picnic lunch out on a blanket.

By this time, my mother had arrived. She suddenly screamed, "Snake!"

Looking up from our lunch preparations, I responded, "No, there is not. I already checked this area out before we set up—"

My voice trailed off as my glance followed my mother's pointing finger to a snake coiled up no more than a foot behind Kay-Kay. As calmly as I could muster, I told Kay-Kay to stand up slowly, then run to me. And she did. She actually obeyed!

Meanwhile, my mother grabbed a stick and quickly killed the snake. It was huge! How had I not seen it? More remarkably, how had not one of the kids stepped on that snake? In all that commotion, why did that snake not uncoil itself and strike my foster daughter, sitting so close by? While it didn't turn out to be venomous, it could still have given her a nasty bite. Had God intervened to protect us from a traumatizing event designed by Satan to hurt us?

During our second year of fostering, Tim accepted a new agricultural sales job that moved us an hour further south. We'd been living in our new home for several months when a wasp infestation began to torment our family. The wasps only appeared at night in the boys' room, not a time when wasps were typically active, crawling onto their beds and stinging them. We could not locate their source, which became increasingly frustrating to the point my children were scared to go to sleep at night.

After much prayer and searching, Tim and I located what we thought must be the wasps' area of entrance, an inside wall that led up to our chimney. Climbing on the roof, I sprayed insecticide down into the chimney. Hundreds of wasps swirled up out of our home, dropping dead to the ground as the poison took effect. I felt we'd gained the victory.

Then just a few weeks later, a pest control technician came to spray for termites and ants. Climbing into a small section of our attic, the man removed a board to spray. He immediately jumped back, screaming. Calling me up to the attic – which was no where near the chimney, he showed me the largest active wasp nest either of us had ever seen— the size of a beach ball! How had these wasps not infested every room in our home? Why had only a few appeared in the boys' room? Was it our prayers that stopped a total invasion of these painful creatures?

Satan's first visible manifestation in Scripture was in the form of a snake when he appeared to Eve in the garden of Eden (Genesis 3). Is it possible that in his attacks against God's children he still chooses to manifest himself through such creatures as snakes or wasps to throw us off balance and cause chaos in our homes? I believe he still does. But for me, this kind of visible battle is the easiest to deal with. As soon as such an attack manifests itself, we usually respond rapidly.

As I look back on each of the above situations, I can see that God permitted evil to be in close proximity so we would turn to him in prayer. His protection was always around us. Just when I would become comfortable in my surroundings and start feeling overconfident, God would allow me to see the dangers in a tangible way that would lead me to offer thanksgiving for his safekeeping, but also to pray for continuous protection from those perils I could not see. Among those threats, I would soon learn, was the foster system itself.

Intensity Level Two: the Bondage of a Dysfunctional System

Saint Francis Xavier, founder of the Jesuits, is credited

with saying:

> "Give me a child until he is seven and anyone may have them afterwards."

Hitler embraced this same philosophy in the brainwashing techniques used by the Nazis for early childhood education. The devil is a dirty fighter, and he too deliberately targets children. Their souls are especially vulnerable to scars and abuse that can traumatize them for life. So as believers, we should be actively advocating for their protection.

One battle we faced during fostering that was less obvious than snakes or wasps was the dysfunction of the court system itself. Caseworkers, judges, and lawmakers might say they wanted what was best for the children. But in the bureaucratic process, children become overlooked and the real victims of a broken system. No child should be left for years in the limbo of never knowing whether they will have a permanent family because their caseworkers are focused on recovery for the parents. But this is exactly how foster care works. The temporary removal of children to a foster home is used by the courts as a motivational tool to inspire the parents to seek help and make different choices. The children are essentially pawns in the process.

How Many Chances Does It Take?

How many chances does it take to prove that a parent is unfit? I remember when I found out our foster kids' birth mom was in jail again just nine months after T-Man and Kay-Kay became part of our family. I was so excited because I believed this would be enough to make clear she wasn't ready to be a full-time mom. But on her court day, the judge gave her six more months to prove herself. I couldn't understand this. Here was a mom so little motivated by the loss of her children that she willingly goes out and commits another felony. Why couldn't the judge see this and release the children from the bondage of being tied to an unfit parent?

The caseworker later excused the light sentence by explaining that her felony was unrelated to the care of her children. Unrelated? How could they be so blind? If she couldn't stay out of jail, she obviously couldn't parent her children! The court system works against itself and in the process, keeps these children and their future in limbo.

How Does This Play Out Spiritually?

There is a real spiritual battle going on for the soul and life of a foster child. The devil does not want to release this child from the system of not belonging. Foster children are continuously bounced between two starkly different worlds: that of their foster parents and that of their birth parents. Confused and pulled in two different directions, their little hearts can become filled with doubt as to who exactly they are and what they will become, leaving them feeling segregated even from a foster family that loves them. This makes them easy prey for the devil.

Even though Satan can also inspire those who are already sold out to him, his power is not without restriction. He can only work within the boundaries permitted by God, and God can use what Satan intends for evil for his own good purposes (Genesis 50:20). Even when a judge is following routine procedures that are not in a child's best interest, he may unknowingly be following God's perfect plan. For instance, during much of our contact with T-Man's and Kay-Kay's birth mom, she was battling suicidal impulses. Did God allow the judge to give her another six months, knowing this small chance would be what ultimately kept her from committing suicide? I may never now, but God does!

Inconsistency of Arbitration

Judges are supposed to listen to all sides of the scenario and make a decision based on the current laws in place. What bothered me greatly was the inconsistency of the process. You would think a case involving the placement of children would be of utmost importance and treated with prodigious respect. At minimum, this should mean that the same judge sentencing the parents to recovery and/or placing their children in foster care should be assigned to every single court date involving their case. Instead, I soon discovered to my great disbelief that there are many judges, and it was a toss-up as to who we would get for any particular court date.

How is the court a spiritual deciding factor? Do the forces of evil work behind the decisions of those who decide the future of these children? Like the saying goes, "The devil is in the details." Every court date filled me with such questions as the following:

Who will be given the authority this time of deciding what happens to my beloved foster children? Will this judge even know their names? Will the caseworker write a report on how well the parents are doing and forget to mention how many times our foster children waited in the car for their parents for a visit only to have to drive home again because no one showed up? Will the district attorney bring up the birth parent's most recent criminal charges? Will the attorney who represents the children (GAL) remember my telephone call about the last disturbing visit they had at their birth parent's home?

God did not design children to be in the middle of a permanency hearing. The current system is broken, leading to immense turmoil and pain for these children as well as their foster parents. Can God bring about good in something so dysfunctional in its very core? Yes, but it will be a fierce battle and one a foster parent must not overlook.

This raging warfare is difficult and treacherous because its claws are entrenched far beyond the problems of a court system. Let's not forget this particular spiritual battle began with two parents influenced destructively by Satan.

From the Voice of Experience:

"When it comes to spiritual battles, it would behoove Christian foster parents to pay close attention to what is going on around their homes. We once had a twelve-year-old foster daughter from a very sad environment of drugs and who knows what else she was exposed to. I began to notice that she had an infatuation with ghosts. She would tell my youngest daughter that our house was haunted. She battled with gender identity, harmful thoughts, and self-harming, and at times we would see her frustration come out in anger.

It was obvious by her discomfort with anything God-related that she was battling spiritual oppression. Fortunately, she never refused to attend church services or activities. Prayer will keep Satan at bay, but unless Christian foster parents really spend time in intercession for little ones like this, Satan may very well prevail. I tried to make sure our family was protected spiritually, but looking back I did not spend time in praying that God would deliver this little girl. The sad part is that she left our home in rebellion and mental anguish. But a few months later she reached out to us through Facebook, apologizing for how she acted and thanking us for loving her. Spiritual warfare in the lives of foster children can never be minimized.

The responsibility of providing and shaping these little one's lives can be overwhelming at times, but let us never forget that "whatever has been born of God conquers the world. This is the victory that has conquered the world: our faith" (1 John 5:4, HCSB). We can help these little ones overcome by showing them

our faith."
—Pastor S.S., foster and adoptive dad.

11 THE DARKEST MOMENT

If you know the enemy and know yourself, you need not fear the result of a hundred battles. If you know yourself but not the enemy, for every victory gained you will also suffer a defeat. If you know neither the enemy nor yourself, you will succumb in every battle.—Sun Tzu, The Art of War

When I think back to my foster children, I can smile despite all the pain. T-Man and Kay-Kay were the good in a very evil situation. They were both miracles, born despite a mother who used drugs while she was pregnant. In the midst of abuse, neglect, and the darkness of drugs, God gave life. God is only one who can create life.

Satan is the total opposite of God. In fact, Jesus himself stated that Satan has been a murderer from the beginning (John 8:44). It may have been Satan's intent for drug addiction and abuse to destroy our foster children's frail lives before they ever entered this world. But God prevailed. Even then, Satan didn't quit. He prompted neglectful parents to be so consumed with drugs that they would not be able to care for their children. But God rescued those children from darkness and placed them in our home.

Did the battle end there? Absolutely not! This next level of intensity illustrates the ongoing effect these birth parents had on their children even after they were placed in our home.

Intensity Level Three: Spiritual Oppression via Our Own Weaknesses

The type of demonic influence termed "spiritual oppression" references being controlled or persecuted by a demonic spirit of darkness. This is not the same as actual demon possession. Satan cannot possess a heart and soul that belongs to Jesus and is indwelt by God's Holy Spirit. However, a believer's personal sin and weaknesses can open the door for Satan to gain a foothold in their lives.

T-Man and Kay-Kay were placed with us due to what was officially termed as abuse and neglect. That general term simply means the parents were not adequately providing for their basic needs of food, clothing and shelter. But beyond neglecting their children's physical needs, we eventually learned that the birth parents' drug abuse generated a lot of violence and fits of rage. This led to multiple incidents of domestic abuse.

Now I know that Christians shouldn't live in fear of Satan and his demonic followers. Because God's Holy Spirit indwelling in us is greater than Satan, we have the power to overcome Satan's attacks (1 John 4:4; 5:5, 18-19). But we must be careful of our past sins, because unconfessed sins are a weak area in which demonic influence can infiltrate our lives and cause chaos. That is what happened in my case.

Even now I am reluctant to share this story, and the memory of it makes me uncomfortable. But in order to illustrate how spiritual warfare can impact even devoted Christians, especially if unconfessed sin has been permitted to fester, I feel called to confess it. This was probably the darkest point of our foster journey. We'd had T-Man and Kay-Kay for 2 ½ years. The birth mom had completely disappeared from the picture due to another relapse and new boyfriend. The birth dad was gradually reappearing, a dad none of us knew.

Meanwhile, my husband had been stressed at his job and I had recently lost my own teaching position, so money was tight. It was winter, and the depressing, gray weather outside mirrored the atmosphere inside our home. To make matters worse, all of the kids had caught the stomach virus.

They took turns throwing up. Each time, I rolled up my sleeves to clean it up until my own body became weak with sickness. I couldn't even find the strength to cook breakfast. Every dish was dirty. Laundry was piled to the ceiling, and I still needed to deal with someone's vomit in the bathtub.

That is when my husband entered the kitchen. Attempting to help, he grabbed a dirty dish and rinsed it out.

"Don't do that!" I reprimanded him feebly but sternly. "Everything needs to be sanitized and run through the dishwasher."

"Well, it's better than nothing!" I heard Tim mutter as he continued rinsing.

In my frustration, I jumped up into Tim's face and began yelling at him for not doing it correctly. I kept nagging at him until he exploded in anger, furiously pushing me away. The push caused me to slip so that I fell, banging my head against the kitchen table. I was startled. Never before had my husband lifted a finger against me. I wasn't really hurt, but in retaliation I jumped up and dialed 9-1-1.

"What is your emergency?" a voice asked me.

I was already regretting my impulsive move, so I hung up. But not ten minutes later a swarm of police cars pulled up outside our home. Then several police officers entered our home to question both Tim and me. It was deeply humiliating.

Fortunately, the female officer questioning me quickly noticed that our entire household was suffering from the stomach flu. She suggested I call someone who wasn't sick to help us. Then as quickly as they'd arrived, the police disappeared, leaving Tim and me still in utter shock as to what had just happened. At that moment, my cell-phone rang. It was our caseworker. He had coincidently driven past our home and seen a ton of cop cars in our driveway. How could this be? His drive to work would not normally take him past our home.

I was beginning to realize this was not just another typical chaotic day. As we talked on the phone, I was completely candid with our caseworker, and I believe God honored that honesty because there were no further repercussions from that police visit. Even more astounding, none of our children had so much as stopped playing during all of that craziness. Nor were any of them traumatized or even particularly impressed by the arrival of so many police officers. I knew it was God who had shielded them from the mess we'd made of that infernal day.

But I also recognized that a demonic spirit I will term Domestic Violence had infiltrated our home and was affecting our family life. Below, I will name other oppressive demonic influences I very clearly sensed in the spiritual warfare that was engulfing our home. I do this in order to identify the kinds of evil we were experiencing. Domestic Violence, for instance, was not something Tim and I had ever struggled with, but I did have unconfessed sins in other areas. These unconfessed sins left a door cracked for Domestic Violence, a demonic influence only too prevalent in our foster children's birth home, to come into our own home.

The most devastating of Satan's attacks are usually the most hidden. One positive result of this terrible incident was to help me recognize that if I did not deal with my own unconfessed sins, I would be consumed and left helpless before the demonic oppression that was assailing our home. So I took action.

Intensity Level Four: the Ultimate Battle of the Mind

After our greatest fight ever, Tim and I could not pretend we were the perfect parents we'd always assumed ourselves to be. I personally had to acknowledge that something was wrong. After a long talk with my husband, I admitted that I had become overly-aggressive. I exploded over simple things. A mess a child had made. A church member asking me not to bring coffee into the sanctuary. Our caseworker rescheduling a visit. Or even my own misperceptions about Tim and his intentions. I would rant and rave, then later feel completely guilty. But no matter how many times I apologized, I felt I could not control these bursts.

I spent time in prayer, asking God to purify my heart from this oppressive demonical spirit of Anger. I had no explanation as to why I felt so angry, but I found multiple references to anger in the Bible. I wrote these down and used them in my daily prayer time (see Appendix for examples). I knew Scripture commanded that I be transformed by the renewing of my mind (Romans 12:2), but I also knew I could not do this on my own. The only way I knew to renew my mind was to saturate it with God's Word. As I did this, it took several months to witness any real change. But in time I no longer found myself exploding.

Where did this spirit of Anger come from? I believe it was an inherited sin. I knew no other way than to get angry when things did not go my way. I had witnessed such reactions while growing up and thought it to be normal. But under deep stress and in the middle of a spiritual fight for young souls previously controlled by the devil, my Anger intensified until it controlled me. I was angry about everything!

A Tip for Foster Parents: Always keep in mind you are in a spiritual battle that necessitates constantly renewing your mind in Christ Jesus.

Whether you are a foster parent, adoptive parent, or a parent at all, always keep in mind you are in a spiritual battle that necessitates constantly renewing your mind in Christ Jesus. This takes intentional effort. It's not just going to happen by asking for it once, then hoping your prayer worked. I learned to fight for what I wanted. I had to exercise my mind in the Bible and be ready to confess deep penetrating sins of my past.

However, the battle within my own mind did not end there. I was still wrestling with spiritual oppression that manifested as various negative emotions. I had already dealt with Fear and Doubt at the beginning of our foster journey. By this point, I no longer experienced fear of the unknown. Nor did I doubt whether God had called us into this journey. But I struggled with other emotions I came to recognize stemmed from demonic influences.

Spirit of Unworthiness

The devil attacked my mind multiple times a week about my lack of worthiness. My mind would accuse me like this:

Who do you think you are? You can't even control your temper! What makes you think you are a good mom? Just look at your life. You're a mess! You will not win this. You do not deserve it. God is not with you. If he was, he would have answered your prayers by now. He does not hear you. You are too sinful, so he has removed his favor over your life. You should just quit now and end the pain you are causing all the kids.

These thoughts of unworthiness would then generate anger, causing me to have an outburst at the kids or my husband. This led to feeling guilty, which would start the thoughts of unworthiness all over again. It was vicious cycle of negativity and darkness. Instead of turning to Scripture, I would indulge in these thoughts. I wallowed in self-pity. I actually enjoyed toying with the idea of quitting.

My face lost its smile, and I would sulk around the house. If something I perceived as "bad" happened, such as the birth dad calling for an extra visit, I would blame myself. I would allow my thoughts to accuse me of being the reason why God's blessing had left our home.

> ***A Tip for Foster Parents: Even though our fight with Satan is invisible – our response to his attack is powerfully visible.***

Our fight with Satan is uniquely invisible. Our response to his attacks is, however, powerfully visible. By humbling ourselves in prayer, we give full power to Christ. This visible action of humility makes Satan sink back in retreat.

> "So humble yourselves before God. Resist the devil, and he will flee from you."
> (James 4:7, NLT)

The devil is tactically very clever, and my mind was his battlefield. I could have easily defeated him and resisted him by remembering who I was in Christ:

- I am salt of the earth and light of the world (Matthew 5:13-14).
- I am a child of God (John 1:12).
- I am holy (I Corinthians 1:2).
- I have the mind of Christ (I Corinthians 2:16).
- I am without blemish and free from accusation (Colossians 1:22).
- I am full of Christ (Colossians 1:27).

As God's children and servants, we are inestimably valuable to God. And because God's Spirit resides within us, we are equipped with power beyond what we could ever comprehend. Just knowing and believing this would have saved me from deep agony and sin as I continued to lash out at my family members and lose self-control of my tongue. But there was another dark spirit I was struggling with that threatened to overwhelm me.

Spirit of Defeat

All along our journey of fostering, I faced great temptation to surrender and give up. Never was it so strong as at the very end. When our journey finally ended with the children being returned to their birth dad, that seemed my ultimate defeat as a foster mom. The devil attacks God's children because it is a way for him to attack God. That is his ultimate target. I can remember so clearly the spirit of Defeat I encountered after our foster children left, even more accusatory and blasphemous than I had ever experienced before:

You lost!?! How can that be? You have no right saying you are a believer and Christ-filled if this is your testimony! No one would want to follow a God who lets one of his children lose this badly! Love did not win. You need to quit. Denounce your Christianity! You should shake your fist at God and never let him control your life again. This is what following him feels like: pain and despair. Quit now and walk free from him who abandoned you and wounded you beyond repair.

It was so easy to believe Satan's lies that I should just throw in the towel in defeat and give up on my faith. While I never got angry with God himself, I did want to quit being called a Christian. We stopped going to church because I begged my husband to let me stay home. I could not face seeing "happy" Christians. I needed time to figure out who God was again despite all the lies flying around in my head.

Summing It All Up

If I could go back in time, I would be more attentive to the unseen playing out in the seen world. It is easier to look back after the fact. That is when we can see how far God has taken us through the fiercest of battles and how he has led us unharmed to victory in the midst of pure evil.

When it comes to spiritual warfare, I didn't face a snakelike form tempting me to eat a forbidden fruit, but I faced an internal evil encounter over the very foundations of my core beliefs as to who God is and what is his place in my life. Ultimately, that is the same temptation Eve faced – and Jesus Himself (Genesis 3; Matthew 4) and it is the same for all of us too. The devil wants us to disown God. He wants us to give in to doubt and remove God's place in our lives as Lord. Do I trust God? Do I believe he is who he says he is? Will I stand by his promises? This is the most intense battle of them all: the battle of belief that fights for control of my heart, soul, and mind.

Some Key reminders of Who God Is:

- God is love (1 John 4:16).
- God is compassionate and gracious, slow to anger and abounding in lovingkindness (Psalm 103:8).
- God is a miracle-working God (Galatians 3:5).
- God is our comforter (2 Corinthians 1:3).
- God is our deliverer (2 Corinthians 1:9-10).
- God is our hope (Psalm 33:20).
- God is a God of peace who defeats our enemies and relieves our troubles (Romans 16:20; 2 Thessalonians 1:6; 1 John 5:4).

From the Voice of Experience:

"It truly is salt on a wound when the verdict is "return

home" [for foster children]. Weekend visits grow longer into overnight stays which melt into permanency. To stay strong as you watch years of love, sacrifice and hope totally disappear is beyond words. The unseen plays itself out by not being able to see what your child may be experiencing, and you will feel it as your family breaks apart. An innocent child will bring back into your home the ways of the world a little more each time, bringing multiple challenges on multiple levels. But trusting God that he knows best is the greatest challenge of them all."
—T.L., foster dad.

12 THE LONG WAY "HOME"

We are called upon not to be successful, but to be faithful.
—Mother Teresa

With the new school year came new challenges. The birth dad was faithful to his court order. He'd made it to all his visits and had now progressed to three-hour unsupervised visits on Saturdays. To add to our frustrations, we had a change of caseworker. I'd been devastated when our prior caseworker took the side of the birth dad in our guardianship hearing. This new caseworker was fresh out of training and had been taught that reunification with birth parents should be pursued at all costs. She told me from the beginning that she wanted to have the children completely reunited with their birth parents within six months, maybe even by Christmas.

I took her words with a grain of salt. After all, we'd been through this before with the birth mom. A lot could still happen before the next scheduled court date in six months. The birth dad would have to stay faithful to his visits, clean from drugs, and out of trouble with the law.

Meanwhile, Kay-Kay was becoming more and more of a struggle even at school, and her new teacher quickly lost patience. When Kay-Kay jammed her pencil into a classmate's arm, she was threatened with suspension. Since the pencil was judged a "weapon", she could even be expelled if the classmate's parents chose to press charges. Thankfully, they made light of the whole situation. But I did feel like the pressures to meet everyone's expectations added significant stress.

At least the other three children were adapting well with the new school year. Both my birth children were receiving rave reviews from their teachers, while T-Man was truly blossoming. Seeing his potential, his teacher removed all his previous IEP labels and put him full time in a regular classroom. I was excited about his future. He needed more help with homework than the others, but all that extra effort was paying off. Academically, all my children were really excelling in school, even Kay-Kay.

But the stress of juggling all the children's needs along with pressure from the agency to begin reunification of our foster children to their birth dad continued to put strain on me.

I've come to understand that when you are called into any difficult spiritual battleground, whether fostering, global missions, church leadership, or in reality any type of ministry, you will soon discover where you are weak. And you can only too quickly fall. It felt to me during this time that not only was the devil working to steal away our foster children, but everything else, including a great husband and a solid, healthy family for my birth kids. I could not allow this!

One friend who had adopted internationally and understood well the stress I was undergoing recommended I try anti-anxiety medication. It had helped her, and my husband agreed it might be worth trying. It sounded like a sure, quick fix. But though I desperately wanted such a fix, I battled with the decision. Here I was trying to rescue children out of the pit of drugs. So what kind of example would I be giving if I became a legal drug user? Drug dependence was still just that—dependence. I didn't want to just *say* I depended on God. I wanted to *live* it.

With that option off my table, I began researching counseling services for foster and/or adoptive parents. Finding one close to our home, I thought I would begin there. After all, I certainly struggled with parenting, and I was again beginning to think that maybe I truly was the problem in our home.

The counselor turned out to have ample experience with fostering and adoption. That counseling was of great benefit to Tim and me, and I would recommend such to every couple who is fostering. The counselor helped us address our weaknesses, teaching me how to stop making myself the scapegoat in every situation and be more forgiving and patient while encouraging Tim to become more engaged and take leadership. Above all, the counseling put us back on the same page as a couple. We were now ready to face the biggest challenge of our lives: our foster children's return home to their birth dad.

> *A Tip for Foster Parents: Counseling is not to be feared but to be used as an effective tool for foster parents to find the strength they may need to continue on the journey.*

The hardest part about long-term fostering is the uncertainty of it all. It would seem easier if God would just reveal to us the time frame. How much longer did I need to endure? It reminded me of how prisoners in WW2 concentration camps must have struggled to keep going. If they'd just known exactly how much longer the war would last, maybe that would have given them the extra strength to endure a bit longer. If I knew just how much longer I had to endure, that might help me fight the daily temptation to call Social Services and ask them to take the children back.

Because that was where I found myself, I did not want to face another year of bouncing the kids back and forth. I did not want to start overnight visits, followed by weekend visits, then holidays. I couldn't handle watching our foster children regress back into their past with every visit.

Nor was it fair to T-Man and Kay-Kay to be in a constant dilemma on how to act. Their birth dad was drastically different than our family. He saw no problem with the children watching R-rated movies and late-night TV shows. He had no stance on bedtime, junk food, cuss words, or media control.

Then there were all the gifts T-Man and Kay-Kay were bringing home. I didn't want to become the sergeant here. I wanted to be the "fun" mom too! But I still had my birth children to think of and protect. I had open conversations with my birth kids when we were alone without T-Man and Kay-Kay about how their birth dad was making up for lost time by showering them with gifts. But I could see my birth kids trying to process all the extra gifts and attention their foster siblings were getting, and I could not make every moment fair and balanced. My birth kids had maturity and understanding beyond their six and eight years of age. But I was worried and exhausted. We could not do this forever. I needed help.

In October 2013, I started pleading with God on behalf of our children, both birth and foster. It broke my heart to watch them all struggle with this unique balancing act of two distinct family dynamics. I've developed great compassion for split families that must do weekend visitations with one parent or the other. Time does not stand still after a divorce. Families move on. Couples remarry and have more kids. Meanwhile, children of the previous marriage are too often left on the outskirts. For them, time has stood still. They have to do the unique dance of managing two separate worlds while not belonging entirely to either.

I begged God for a clear answer that would bring relief to our situation. I also asked God to reveal to me how much longer. As I prayed, I received a distinct revelation from God's Holy Spirit: *only until the end of this year*. That meant only three more months!

With this revelation, my spirit was lifted. It changed the way I viewed my whole situation. No longer was I going to become these foster children's permanent mother. I was currently little more than a babysitter. With that in mind, Kay-Kay's misbehavior became easier to manage. I do believe that in those final months, she sensed me pulling away emotionally, and I believe her misbehavior was just her way of grieving. She had no other way of expressing it.

We were honest with the children and tried our best to prepare T-Man and Kay-Kay for their new home with their dad and his girlfriend. I was concerned that Kay-Kay would be without a mother figure once again. I could no longer provide that maternal protection and bonding she so desperately needed.

At least at the time we were going through this process, Social Services in our area offered no real transition or therapy to prepare kids for reunification. The attitude seemed to be that children are resilient and can handle everything. All they need is reunification with their birth parents. In consequence, the way foster children too often process the road trip of returning "home" is often through regression and disobedience.

For Kay-Kay, she started waking up at night. She would kick the walls. She would play instead of sleep. She would walk around the house. This really concerned me. My prayer life intensified. I switched her to a bedroom close to ours. I didn't get much sleep. But I could handle this because I knew it was only for a little longer.

By November, the caseworker increased visitation to overnight weekend visits. She would pick the kids up from school on Fridays and take them directly to their birth dad's house. She would return them to us on Sunday evening. Her goal was to prove by our next court date that the foster children were ready to be permanently reunited with their parents. That court date was now less than a month away on December 18th. So she had just three weekends to document that the birth dad was ready to be a serious, full-time, forever parent.

I remember well that first overnight visit with the birth

dad. He and a teenage daughter from another marriage lived with his girlfriend, her adult son, and her teenage daughter. Our foster children had to leave an environment of all young children to adjust to a teenage/adult environment. Here is a small insert from my journal:

> *November 22-23 was the kids' first overnight visit with Daddy X. They were exhausted when they came back. The first overnight weekend was hard on us all. But Kay-Kay has shown a lot of affection upon returning which means, I guess, she does love me! T-Man is the one who is adjusting the hardest. He said he can't sleep at his dad's; it's too scary. So we are packing light-up toys for next weekend. Then he told me he can't go because he has itchy feet and his dad has no medicine for kids. So, now spray medicine is packed. Then he said his dad didn't have any kids' DVDs and Superman is not a kid movie. SO, we packed up kids' movies, clothes, toys and half of our kid books. Kay-Kay told me she doesn't like to sleep there either because they say bad words. I asked, "Really, what did they tell you?" She said, "They told me 'SHUT UP'!" Oh boy, I thought. This is going to be a rough transition!*

To those witnessing our story, it may appear that we surrendered easily to the will of the court. The truth is, I did not go down without a fight. I talked with five different lawyers. I paid one of these to represent us. It was wasted money since foster parents have no legal rights. I petitioned the court through letters to the judge and district attorney (DA). I left the DA and our foster children's GAL (guardian at large) countless voice messages. I called supervisors and even board members of the social service agency.

> *A Tip for Foster Parents: In Illinois, a foster parent can be granted 'intervenor status' after a child is placed with them for over a year (some states are much less). A foster parent can also request the court to assign a CASA worker to the case for an unbiased voice in the court.*

We also filled out the paperwork to be granted "intervenor status", which would permit us to advocate in court on behalf of what we believed was in the best interests of our foster children instead of whatever the caseworker chose to advocate, as was our current situation as foster parents. But despite all my frenzied efforts, God had another plan for us and our foster children. I am glad I fought hard for the kids. I did all I could do to keep them with us. But as fall faded and winter took over, it was clear that the battle was ending. I did not have to fight anymore.

Our final court date arrived on December 18, 2013, and with it, surprisingly, came peace. As I always did, I prayed before entering the courthouse that God would be the true Judge who gives the verdict. I asked God to allow us to see him controlling and orchestrating this case and not the agency, judge, or attorneys. I visualized the angels I knew would be with us unseen in the courtroom. I prayed that my behavior and attitude would reflect the God I love.

It went exactly as I'd prayed. A new judge I had not seen before entered the courtroom. Both birth parents were present, a surprise since the birth mother had dropped out of visits and the reunification case for almost a year now. The attorneys present spoke in favor of the birth parents, after which the caseworker gave a glowing report on the successful recovery of the birth dad. The judge then officially finalized the reunification. She praised and cautioned the birth dad to continue staying away from drugs so he could be the dad he was intended to be. She told the birth mom not to give up.

The judge even acknowledged us. Like flies on a wall, foster parents are often given no recognition unless the case becomes an adoption proceeding. But she praised us, stating that Tim and I must be the reason this case had turned out so beautifully. I cried through the entire process, tears of relief and true sadness that the journey was indeed finally over.

After the court was dismissed, I walked to the front of the room and thrust out my hand towards the man I'd previously thought of as my enemy—the district attorney who six months ago could have granted our petition to become adoptive parents, but whose advocating instead for the birth dad was the reason we were no longer even foster parents. He looked taken aback as I shook his hand.

"Thank you for your involvement in this case," I told him. "And your suggestions not to terminate parental rights back in August. It is because of your insistence that our foster children will be shortly reunited with their dad. I must admit how deeply hurt and angry I felt back in August. You had all the power and voice to grant our dream of adopting two precious children who have bonded to us and whom we view our own. However, I agree that reunification does seem to be what is really best for these children now. Despite our pain, I believe you made the right decision because reunification is a beautiful outcome."

He thanked me sincerely for my words. The date for T-Man's and Kay-Kay's return home was set for December 26th, the birth dad graciously allowed the children to stay with us through one more Christmas. With permission from the dad and caseworker, we planned the biggest celebration/family memory we could possibly afford—a trip to Disney World.

Before we left for Disney World, we held a special

family church service similar to a baby dedication ceremony. My dad officiated, praying God's blessing over our foster children and dedicating them to the Lord. My daughter Faith and I sang a song together. Our entire extended family each laid hands on T-Man and Kay-Kay, praying for God's protection over them. Many tears were shed along with songs of joy for the gift God had given us in having T-Man and Kay-Kay in our lives for three years.

> *A Tip for Foster Parents: When a foster child returns to the birth parents, plan a special family celebration of thanksgiving for the time granted to you by God.*

Let me just add here how incredibly vital I've come to see that it is to celebrate with our foster children before they return home, no matter how heartbroken we may be. Yes, we may mourn and that is good. However, we should do everything possible to make those last days and moments shine in their memories. We need to celebrate God's goodness that brought our lives together however briefly but meaningfully.

This doesn't mean a celebration must be as extravagant as we did with Disney. In fact, our circumstances were unusual as it is rare to get permission to take foster children out-of-state, and usually once the decision is made by the court, the time frame for returning home is fast. But celebrating does need to be commemorative and fun. Maybe a big, colorful "I Love You Because" farewell party where words of thanksgiving are shared and prayers of dedication or a family outing to some place special like the zoo or an amusement park. These are just some ways to leave a lasting positive memory with these children as they return to what may be a difficult situation. They will cherish the last moments spent together.

On December 20th, we all flew out of St Louis to Orlando, Florida. This would be our foster kids' first time on an airplane, first time at the beach, and first time to Disney World. We wanted this often-painful journey to end on the happiest, fun-filled note possible. It was truly a treat God gave to us. Even providing the finances to lavish this kind of celebration on the children was a miracle. We spent one day at Disney World, a day at Gatorland, and three days on the beach, jumping waves, collecting shells, and eating shrimp pizza in the beachside hotel.

Even now looking back, we all remember this trip as the best vacation of all times. The kids didn't fight once, and though we felt melancholy, we also felt thankful. What made it so special? Was it the relief of a chapter closing after the immense pain we'd all suffered? The enchantment of new firsts even while it was our last outing all together as a family?

Christmas in Disney World is everywhere. Fake snow falls from the sky. There are free cookies at each booth. Choirs carol the angel chorus: "Peace on earth, goodwill towards all men." As I soaked in the holiday atmosphere, my spirit wrestled with this peace the angels had promised.

It is what the angels said, I recognized. *It was promised. It was delivered in the person of Jesus Christ. Just like Jesus told his own disciples when they were grieving because he was about to leave them:*

> "Peace I leave with you; my peace I give you. I do not give to you as the world gives. Do not let your hearts be troubled and do not be afraid."
> (John 14:27)

But how do I tap into that peace? Especially now in this time of parting and for the future when T-Man and Kay-Kay will no longer be with us. How does my heart rest knowing I am not there to protect and comfort and pray for these children ever again?

I didn't have any perfect answers. But as we all sat on the beach watching the warm sun set over stunning turquoise waters on that last evening, I felt God's peace settle over us. For Tim and me, that included the peace of a job well done. T-Man's and Kay-Kay's path might be splitting from ours in the morning, but this story was never our story. It's God's story, and it is he who determines the end.

From the Voice of Experience:

"I had to come to terms and accept my part in the journey of fostering. I asked the Lord to show me what that looked like because I knew it might be different than what I wanted. Right before it was time to send off the foster children that had been with us for so long back to their birth mom, our foster son prayed, thanking the Lord that he had gained us as a family. It opened my eyes to see that by returning home to his mom he wasn't losing us, he was gaining a whole new family!"

—S.G. foster mom.

13 LOSS AND GRIEF

Don't cry because it's over; smile because it happened.
—Dr. Seuss

When one door of happiness closes, another opens; but often we look so long at the closed door that we do not see the one which has been opened for us. —Helen Keller

On Christmas Day 2013, after five days of wonderful family vacation in balmy Florida, we all boarded the plane to fly back to the freezing winter of southern Illinois. As we landed in St Louis, MO, the closest airport to our small town, the reality of having to return T-Man and Kay-Kay to their birth dad in just a few hours overwhelmed my spirit. Upon arriving home, I immediately began packing up their clothes and other last-minute items. As I did so, T-Man kept coming in to wrap his arms around my neck, filling me with questions and concerns beyond my abilities to solve. Poking through the boxes, he would pick up an item and say, "Remember when—?"

I had to keep fighting back tears. I would miss him so much! Meanwhile, Kay-Kay bounced from room to room. All this new chaos was thrilling to her little being. I knew I'd miss her tenacious spirit. The house would be awfully quiet without her.

My birth children, Caleb and Faith, were playing the new board games they'd received for Christmas. Tim and I had decided to make the best of this day by allowing all the kids to open their gifts as soon as we arrived back from the airport. We'd hoped the toys would distract them all from my packing up of our foster children's belongings. But only Caleb and Faith played with a meditative calmness. T-Man seemed depressed and distant. Kay-Kay danced around excitedly. It was as though each child sensed something terrifyingly new was waiting just around the corner.

Early the next morning, we loaded our pickup truck with all of T-Man's and Kay-Kay's belongings along with other items that might help them adjust to their new and unfamiliar home. Then the six of us piled into the truck. Thankfully, our caseworker had given permission for all of us to go, since my birth kids wanted to see where their foster siblings were going and who would be their new family. Once we were loaded, Tim prayed for our trip and for God's special blessing over T-Man and Kay-Kay.

The hour-long drive passed mostly in silence. Kay-Kay was giddy and smiling as though this were all some big game, but T-Man, Caleb, and Faith looked scared and sad. Tim tried to act lighthearted, pointing out cows, barns, and anything else that might distract the kids. T-Man began insisting he didn't want to go. Caleb and Faith calmly reassured him that his birth daddy loved him and wanted him at his house. But T-Man couldn't relax. I don't remember saying much. Inside, I was praying and distraught.

When we arrived, the birth dad's entire family as well as the caseworker were there to welcome the kids. As we toured the house, my heart plummeted even further. Kay-Kay's room was a small closet that opened into the attic where her teenage step-sisters slept on mattresses spread directly on the floor. I began to imagine all the immorality my innocent foster daughter might learn from teenage girls who had no restrictions as to their boyfriends, language, and lifestyle. Even worse, the only way up to the attic was through the birth dad's girlfriend's adult son's room. Such would never be permitted in a foster home!

T-Man did have his own room downstairs. It was of a decent size, and he even had his own TV. Despite my fears and concerns, I could see the parents made a special effort to decorate with the kids' favorite toys and that the entire family was excited to have Kay-Kay and T-Man "home" again. This comforted me to some level.

After the tour, their birth dad begged us to stay and watch Kay-Kay and T-Man open their Christmas gifts. Seeing the environment my foster children would face for the rest of their lives was already torture for me. I didn't want to watch them opening an entire second set of gifts, especially since my birth kids had to stand there processing all that was going on. But we stayed. Sadly, as T-Man and Kay-Kay tore open their gifts, they immediately began quarreling: "Don't touch that! Gimmie that! It's mine!"

Meanwhile, Tim, the kids, and I were feeling distinctly out of place as we just stood around gawking. I was astonished at how much money these parents clearly had to lavish on costly gifts. It felt like a big show to impress the social worker and bribe the children. Once the gifts were all opened, Kay-Kay and T-Man busied themselves with their new toys, completely ignoring Caleb and Faith. So we quickly prepared to leave. T-Man refused to say goodbye to me. He would not hug me or look at me in the eye.

I bent down and gave him a hug, whispering, "I love you. Always trust Jesus."

He gave me no response, but he did give my birth kids a hug goodbye. I could see Caleb and Faith were unhappy, but I am thankful they have this memory of saying goodbye. Kay-Kay squealed and giggled as I hugged her and told her I loved her.

"I love you too," she responded hurriedly, but with no real emotion in her voice. She dismissed me hastily to return to playing with her new toys. I turned and ran out of the house before my tears could spill over. Shaking with grief, I climbed into our truck to wait for Tim, Caleb, and Faith.

The birth dad had witnessed my distressed departure. Hurrying outside to our truck, he assured me Kay-Kay and T-Man would always be part of my life. "We are family now. For every birthday you and your family will be invited. We will do picnics in the summer. We will go to church together for Christmas and Easter."

I nodded my head and thanked him. But God had already revealed to me that his assurances were not true. As we drove off, I knew I would not be allowed back into their home, much less their lives. Over the following days, I tried my best to be thankful for my family as it was. I didn't want Caleb and Faith thinking they were not enough.

Grief is a funny thing. You want to cry over the loss, and you need to, but sometimes that confuses those who love you and want you happy. I didn't want my unhappiness to be misinterpreted. I deeply loved my birth children. I was immensely thankful for them. But I did miss my foster children.

Confusion and sorrow quickly led to depression. Simple household tasks would make me cry as I remembered my loss. For example, not running the dishwasher twice a day because we didn't have as many dirty dishes. Or running out of dirty laundry to wash and put away. My van now had empty seats on the drive to school.

Once Caleb and Faith had returned to school and Tim to his work, I felt alone and lacking in purpose for my life. Even with more counseling, I found myself constantly depressed. I was not angry at God but at myself. I believed the lie that God had removed T-Man and Kay-Kay from our home because I was unworthy as a parent. Why else would God take them from a home that loves God to be placed in an unbelieving home?

I also told myself the only reason God hadn't taken away Caleb and Faith too was because of Tim's goodness as a parent. Since I couldn't figure out the whys behind losing our foster kids, I determined that *I* had to be the problem. Which sent me into an even deeper despair. When a person feels that they are the problem, it is hard for them to find a solution to that problem on their own.

My husband loves me deeply. He was patient with me for a couple weeks. Then he sat me down and painted an honest picture of me. I never got out of my pajamas, something I hadn't even noticed. I was lying on the couch all day and sleeping too much at night. He begged me to notice him and the children. I told him I was sincerely trying. And I was.

Then Tim asked me to dream. Dream? I couldn't remember the last time I had taken time to dream beyond the dream of adopting our foster children. Before Tim and I were married, we'd often sit together and dream. The dreams we talked about and goals we set for ourselves were idealistic, even out of reach. But by God's grace, we'd worked hard and had accomplished many of our dreams.

But during this lengthy process of fostering, I had stopped dreaming. I'd thought fostering and adopting *was* my dream. For years that was all my life had been about, and with that dream gone, I really didn't know where to go next. Did God want me to go back to teaching? Or maybe he was calling our family into overseas missions? Had God returned our foster children home so we could travel across international borders, as we couldn't while they were in our care?

After many tears and deep soul searching, I told my husband I needed to go back to the land where I'd grown up, Bolivia. My memories of Bolivia were of a land hungry and thirsty for Christ as well as Christians on fire for God. Santa Cruz, our home town there, was a bustling, lively city in Bolivia's lowland jungle zone with tropical warmth year around, natural foods, and laid-back, friendly people.

And surely my current self-centered outlook on life would dissipate once I was reminded of the overwhelming poverty and never-ending needs that were also in my memories of Bolivia. I could show Caleb and Faith where I grew up. I could introduce my family to all my Bolivian friends, with whom I'd maintained contact over the years.

We could all try new foods and soak up the sun, January being summer south of the equator. Maybe in Bolivia I would find my answers.

Tim readily agreed to spending ten days in Bolivia visiting mission agencies, friends, missionaries, churches, schools, hospitals, any place with open ministry opportunities. This was our children's first international flight, and it became a bonding experience for our family as we adventured into new places, tried new foods, met new people. We even flew to Sucre, another Bolivian city high in the Andes mountains with a culture left-over from Inca times. We interviewed with missionaries and prayed with friends to see if God was calling us to Bolivia. I began to be hopeful we had found our new calling.

Being with my Bolivian friends again contributed greatly to my healing. One dear friend from high school listened patiently, then told me about her own losses through miscarriage. But after a couple days of bonding, she told me frankly, "You have let yourself go! Where is your make-up? Pretty clothes? You still have a husband to please. A home to build. Let me help you."

Opening her purse right then and there, she put make-up on my face, brushed my hair, and painted my nails. She told me I was beautiful and reminded me that this moment of loss did not define me.

A Bolivian pastor from my childhood we were visiting also prayed over me with such intensity we both began to cry. Embracing me, his wife reminded me that I needed to trust God as the true Father of our foster children. Even if I cannot be with them, he will still protect them.

With such encouragement, we returned home fired up to start whatever new mission to which God was calling us. We had already listed our home for sale, and it sold in just two weeks. We were sure at first that God would be sending us overseas. But after we'd knocked on numerous doors, God made clear to us that we were to stay in Illinois.

We ended up buying a twenty-seven-acre farm with a small 140-year-old house on it just ten miles down the road from our previous home. This permitted our children to keep in contact with their former school friends. My time and energy went into fixing up our new home and caring for the farm animals. I also started homeschooling my children. The farm setting was peaceful, and in teaching my children God's Word I found new purpose and meaning for my life.

Cycle of Grief

When I look back now over this time of loss, I can see clearly the stages I passed through that I call the cycle of grief: memory of sadness, anger, blaming, purpose, hopefulness.

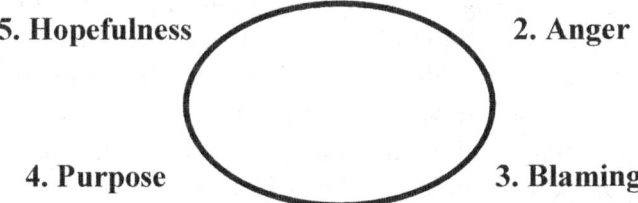

I would be going about my usual day when a sudden memory of my foster children would pop into my head, triggering an intense sadness that would then lead to me being angry at how the whole deal went down. My anger would cool as I began blaming myself or the dysfunctional system for our loss. As the blame game in turn subsided, I would search desperately for some new purpose that would justify and give meaning to our loss (overseas missions, for instance, which we couldn't do with foster kids). Once I could conjure up a purpose, I could feel hopeful that everything was going to be okay.

Then some simple thing would throw me back into stage one of remembering and sadness. One such was when the Social Services agency called to say they could not approve our recently purchased old farmhouse as a foster home so I would need to surrender our foster license. The licensing representative tried to reassure me that if we ever built onto our current residence, they would approve us. But it felt as though our possibility of ever adopting and increasing our family were over. Could it be that God's calling for us to be foster parents had only been for three short years and to a single set of siblings?

Other reminders of loss came when friends who were also fostering to adopt texted about their progress or upcoming adoption. To be excited for them yet saddened at never achieving that goal for myself was a crazy mix of emotions.

At first, I would go through this cycle almost daily. But as time passed and with God's help, I found myself recovering and being more hopeful than any of the other stages. I liked being hopeful. To be hopeful is to dream.

Each day I had the habit of walking to a hill on our small farm that overlooked where our animals grazed. There I would pray that God would bless our farm and make it fruitful. One day I remember clearly hearing God's voice tell me, *"Pray that over your body."*

I argued a bit with God about the practicality and reality of that prayer. "My tubes are tied, remember? I will never experience pregnancy again. Our foster license is gone. Adoption is out of the question without an approved home. God, what are you asking of me?"

But in confirmation of God's command, I had a dream just a short time later in which I saw Caleb and Faith playing with a baby on our front lawn. As a second confirmation, my husband (who normally doesn't dream, period!) woke up one night out of the blue, hugged me, and told me he'd dreamt of having a baby. He went on to say he wanted to try for another baby. Like Abraham's wife Sarah when God told Abraham she'd finally have a baby at ninety years of age (Genesis 18:12), I laughed at the thought of being pregnant again.

"I guess that means you dreamed of a different wife too!" I answered him sarcastically.

But in my daily quiet time with God, I began asking God what it was he wanted me to be asking of him. And each time I asked, I began pleading for a child. My quiet times would go on for hours, and I would cry out to God for the opportunity to be pregnant even while I knew the possibility of a child was completely foolishness. I trusted with all my heart that God could do a miracle if he chose.

Again, I was just trying to be obedient to what God was asking of me. I didn't understand what God had in mind, and I didn't know how God would accomplish this in my life. I was just trusting. The more I trusted, the more I grew to love God and leave behind the bitterness loss had created. Trusting God is knowing him personally. The more you know him, the easier it is to trust him. Visualize a small child being led by the hand of her loving Father. It's that simplicity of trust that eliminates the bitterness of not knowing all the *whys* in life.

> *A Tip for Foster Parents: Simple trust that comes by knowing God eliminates the void created by all the uncertainties that come with loss.*

And as God led me, he healed me emotionally. Now I could be ready for what he had next for Tim and me—a physical healing.

From the Voice of Experience:

"Dear God, you probably know how I feel and that I just really miss them and that I don't know how to explain it. Please God, I need your help. I know that the Bible says I'll get rewarded, but really, I can't stop thinking about them. Should I write to them, or should I wait until I'm older, or just pray? Amen."
—Faith Lewis, age 8, a year after our foster children returned to their home.

14 A DIFFERENT POINT OF VIEW

Children are the living messages we send to a time we will not see.—President John F. Kennedy

As I walked out the door toward the gate that would lead to my freedom, I knew that if I did not leave all the anger, hatred, and bitterness behind I would still be in prison.
—Nelson Mandela

Tis better to have loved and lost than never to have loved at all.—Alfred Lord Tennyson

My birth children have been amazing troopers throughout our foster journey. Not only did they have to share their rooms, clothing, and personal space, but the love and attention from their parents, grandparents, and extended family. Even Christmas and birthday celebrations had to be divided between four instead of two, which meant fewer gifts.

And yet when I've questioned my children as to their feelings regarding our foster journey, I've been astounded that neither even brought up the sacrifices they had to endure. I wanted to share some of my children's thoughts as they look back onto our foster care experience.

Caleb

Caleb is of a quiet nature and a deep thinker but very tenderhearted. These are his words at age twelve:

"My best part about being a foster sibling was having another brother and sister. Some great memories I have are of climbing trees together, four-wheel riding and mudding together, teaching T-Man to shoot my BB guns, racing canoes with him, and all of us kids swimming in our pool. I always remember T-Man as a happy kid. He really liked to play.

"The worst part about fostering was having to share them on weekends with their birth parents. And of course, when they left us permanently. That first year they were gone, I thought about them all the time. I realized I missed teaching T-Man when I was alone in the woods playing. I no longer had a friend beside me.

"I am glad my parents fostered because that is what God told them to do. I do think one day I will see my foster siblings again. God showed this to me in a dream. I dreamed I saw T-Man at a church function. There were big blow-up bouncy houses and balloons, and everyone was having fun. I saw him, and he saw me. We were like, "Hey!" Then we were friends again just like before he left."

Faith

Faith is a full-throttle kind of girl. She loves people with everything in her and never holds back. But when you love generously, you can also easily get hurt. Here are some of her thoughts at age eleven on our fostering:

"The first thing I remember about our foster siblings was setting all of Kay-Kay's gifts for her on her bed before she even arrived. I remember when they did arrive that they looked sad and scared. My mom told me to give them some space. But, of course, I did not listen. I just ran to them immediately and began to play with them.

"My best moments I can remember in fostering are Kay-Kay and me having an ice-cream competition. Sometimes after school Mommy would take us to Dairy Queen and buy us ice-cream cones. Kay-Kay loved ice-cream and was very good at eating it faster than anyone else. I also remember having a chili hot dog competition with T-Man. He won, of course. T-Man was so good at catching things even though he had a weak hand, like frogs, live fish, once even a wild rabbit.

"My worst memories are of Kay-Kay and me fighting. I specifically remember one of our first fights where we were standing in line to brush our teeth. We were fighting about who was first, and she bit me. Well, I bit her back. My mom ended up putting us both in time out in the kitchen.

"My advice for foster siblings is that you need to be ready to give lots of love and have lots of patience. Loving may mean that you will experience pain. It's worth the pain though. Because you can't break love no matter how much the pain is. Love is always stronger.

> *A Tip for Foster Parents: No matter how intense the pain is, love is always stronger.*

"I would have been able to handle the first year my foster siblings were gone better if I could have seen them more. It really hurt that I never received an answer to my letters and cards. Even so, I would still do fostering again. And I would do fostering as an adult when I grow up if I have the chance.

"I think it is important to foster because it is a good way to tell people you love Jesus. Even though our foster siblings may not be where they can hear about Jesus every day, Jesus is somewhere still in their hearts. It helps to have people around you to remind you about Jesus. They may not have that right now where they are living. But we did get to share Jesus with them, and that won't just disappear. I do hope I get to see them in the future.

Tim

I asked Tim to comment also on our three-year venture. While my husband is a man of few words, he is an excellent communicator, and I really treasure his insight. Here are some of his thoughts:

"I would define our three-year process of fostering as rewarding. It was rewarding to watch children have corn on the cob and fresh strawberries for the first time. It was rewarding to show them what a water park was. It was rewarding to watch their grades improve in school and to help their confidence grow. Though it was also challenging to blend two very different worlds together. Our expectations for their behavior were hard for them to meet because at such a young age they had already learned to become self-reliant and they did not have the maturity to sort all that out.

"The most challenging part of the whole experience was dealing with the foster system. From the initial phone call [notifying of a foster placement] to the last court date, foster parents are given very little regard in the eyes of the system and the courts. The biological parent who is a recovering heroin addict sees more value in the bond the children had with us then the trained professionals. Through the course of three years, multiple social workers, nurses, and supervisors are making life-impacting decisions for innocent children when they don't even know their full names, their favorite colors, likes or dislikes. This includes ordering these children to have to visit rehab centers, prisons, and the like. What foster children overcome in life is beyond description.

"If I could go back and relive that foster experience, what I'd do differently would be to trust God that the outcome is truly in his hands and he knows best. I would treat each day as a gift given to me to share love and joy. I would encourage our birth children just to enjoy the experience and not worry about tomorrow. I would try to be more honest and open with our birth children about what the outcome may or may not be. I would try not to let them feel the tension that is involved with all the chaos. I would try to focus on the laughter instead of all the challenges.

> *A Tip for Foster Parents: Each day is a gift given to you to share love and joy.*

"I believe if you feel the call or the tug on your heart to foster, you should do so. It may be the only consistency those foster children ever get to experience, even if it is for a short time. Any love and kindness you can share is advantageous for everyone involved. Don't let the classes and other requirements scare you off. And try to have compassion for the social workers. We all need to understand that the caseworker's hands are tied in most areas and that they have a lot of hoops to jump through just to survive.

"Also, try your best to attend any and all court dates. It is there you will see the true status of the case. I'd encourage anyone wanting to foster to do all they can to connect with the biological parents. It really is in the best interest of the children to see unity at that level. If you can, go to all the visits the system will allow you to attend. This one effort will allow for some consistency in the foster children's life, and it is here where you will build unity with the birth parents. Learn to put others before yourself.

"I can honestly say that when we did get to the end of fostering, when our foster children went to live with their dad, I was glad. I was relieved that it was all over. There would be no more stress of having to deal with visits, regression in behavior, caseworkers, kids fighting, or an upset wife. But as time passed, I wasn't glad anymore. I was hurt. I felt jaded. I felt like we had been cheated. It just didn't seem fair. Even though I knew God was directing our paths, I still wrestled with where life was going. Sometimes your heart and your head are far apart from each other. Most of the time, you will find yourself dragging your heart along.

"Even so, all of us should strive to protect the innocent. But protection of the innocent has multiple meanings to the multiple people involved. You need to know when you accept the phone call to foster that reunification is the goal regardless of what anyone may tell you. It would be beneficial to keep that in mind for yourself as well as for your birth children and for your foster children."

From the Voice of Experience:

"I was concerned with how my grandchildren were impacted by the decision of fostering. While the foster children got special gifts and attention, my grandkids were not given the same treatment. It was exhausting to think about all the medical and dental visits, parental visits, and caseworker visits the children endured along with all the attention of the visits.

The foster children may become accustomed to the attention and come to expect it. The risk here is that they can become "lifers" to the system itself, always seeking attention through counselors and support systems without becoming independent and mature. The goals and objectives are different and at times opposite as foster parents may want to adopt, while the system has reunification with the family of origin as their first priority. Someone needs to tell the truth; it will set everyone free."

—C.E., grandparent to a foster family.

15 JOURNEY TO A MIRACLE

There is a unique pain that comes from preparing a place in your heart for a child that never comes.—David Platt

Every experience God gives us, every person he puts in our lives, is the perfect preparation for a future only he can see.
—Corrie Ten Boom

When you want something but can't have it, you begin to notice it all around you. Everywhere I went—the zoo, the park, the school, the hospital—I spotted pregnant women. Female acquaintances were announcing their pregnancies. Even my animals were pregnant. While I was in constant prayer and had faith that God could give Tim and me another baby, I kept receiving the usual monthly reminder that I was still not pregnant.

I've mentioned before the story of Sarah, wife of the biblical patriarch Abraham (chapters 12-23 of Genesis). She'd grown tired of waiting for God to keep his promise of giving Abraham a son, which is why she'd offered up her slave, Hagar, to Abraham (Genesis 16). And it wasn't just a few years of waiting. Abraham was seventy-five years old when God first told him he would father many nations and a hundred years old when Sarah finally bore him a son, Isaac. That's a grand total of twenty-five years of waiting.

Scripture seems to indicate that Sarah had already reached menopause since the apostle Paul references Sarah's womb as "dead" in his epistle to the Romans (Romans 4:19). I knew nothing was impossible for God, but I was already thirty-four years old, and I really didn't want to be a ninety-year-old woman trying to jiggle a baby on my hip. Nor could I see Tim being patient with a crying baby at night much past his forties!

However, this was God writing our story, and his ways are far above our ways. So I tried to busy myself with different ministries to keep my mind off my longing for another child. One day I was chatting with our pastor's wife, who was pregnant with her third child. I knew she had struggled with infertility and had conceived her two previous children through In Vitro Fertilization, or IVF. Gathering up my courage, I asked her if this pregnancy was also through IVF. She graciously explained the process of her third successful IVF. She also explained that to use up all her harvested embryos, which had been cryogenically frozen, she would go through the process one more time.

Our discussion led me to begin praying over and researching the possibility of adopting a frozen embryo. I discovered that since not all embryos—i.e., fertilized eggs—resulting from IVF are implanted in the biological mother, hundreds of thousands remain frozen in fertility clinics. Many of these are available for what is termed embryonic adoption, i.e., the placing of that embryo in the womb of an adoptive mother. What a special way to save the unborn! It seemed to me that embryonic adoption would fulfill two of my deep desires—the wish for a new child living inside of me and adoption.

While I had begun researching for a center that could do embryonic adoption at a decent price, my husband was not totally on board. After all the pain we'd endured in fostering, he wanted to make sure that no biological mom or dad could eventually appear to snatch our child away. He also brought up the matter of costs. Going online to the website of a center I was checking out, I pulled up the pricing information. That is when I spotted in the price listings something I'd never even noticed was also on that center's website—Tubal Reversal (TR) surgery!

I hadn't even considered that reversing my tubal ligation might be a possibility. As I read, I immediately recognized that TR was not only more affordable with a higher chance of success, but would not load me up with potentially harmful drugs I would have to take for an embryonic adoption. When I presented my discovery to my husband, he sighed with relief. His immediate approval confirmed for me that we had found what God wanted us to do.

The center Tim and I chose for the TR surgery was in North Carolina: A Personal Choice with Dr. Monteith. I filled out paperwork, did bloodwork, and was placed on a waiting list. Just one week later I received a call that the date of December 10th, 2014, was available for the surgery. I accepted. In less than one month and almost to the year since losing our foster children, I would be having a Tubal Reversal.

The doctor performing the TR informed me that chances of a successful pregnancy for a woman my age and weight were about 75%. But he would not know fully what my chances of success were until he saw how much of my fallopian tubes had been cut away in the original ligation. Reversing the ligation required long enough tubes to sew back together. But he was hopeful, and I took encouragement from that.

On the chilly Illinois winter morning of December 10th, I woke up early, fearful and anxious. For the surgery, I would be put under anesthesia. Part of the paperwork had included signing away liability in case of death. Faith in God is like that. When I made a commitment to love the Lord my God with all my heart and to give my life to God to do with it as he pleases, I signed away all liability and entrusted my whole being to my Creator.

I'd never have guessed that one day I'd be here ready to have some strange doctor reopen my body and stitch my tubes back together. Following our Creator is like that too. He leads us down paths that are unknown and unpredictable. Trusting him is an adventure. Trusting takes practice. It is not a natural thing to do. It is a daily exercise.

I was so nervous before the surgery I had to keep praying for God's peace. During Christmas 2013, I had prayed for peace amidst uncertainty and loss. Now here I was a full year later still praying for peace. I asked Jesus to calm me and reassure me that this idea of a Tubal Reversal was his idea and not just mine. My heart was racing, and an inner voice tried to persuade me to quit again: *The risk may not be worth the reward. What about your two children at home? If you die, who will be a mother to them? Why are you never content?*

But as I continued to pray, the confusion and anxiety left me, and my spirit began to relax. A Bible verse that was the words of Jesus himself came to me:

> When a woman gives birth, she has a hard time, there's no getting around it. But when the baby is born, there is joy in the birth. This new life in the world wipes out the memory of the pain. (John 16:21, MSG)

Sure enough, once we arrived at the clinic, everything worked like clockwork. The doctor administering anesthesia started a countdown: "One . . . two . . ." That was as far as I remember. I awoke to find Tim holding my hand and telling me it was all over. The doctor came in with a huge smile. He proceeded to tell me a lot of technical and scientific jargon, but all I heard was, "Congratulations! You have a 90% chance of success."

The doctor went on to explain that he'd rarely seen so little of the fallopian tubes removed as had been the case in my original ligation. Typically, a doctor removes 1-3 centimeters from the tube's average 8-12 centimeters of length. The doctor who'd delivered my last child, Faith, and done the tubal ligation had only removed 0.7 centimeters, which meant that my chances now were extremely promising. I breathed a sigh of thankfulness and relief.

I was now living once again with hope. Without hope, I'd felt dejected like a wilting, dying plant. I had exhausted myself in the journey of fostering. I had believed the lie that God could not use me as a mother to the fatherless, much less carry another baby in my womb. Hope makes one come alive again. When a person has hope, the Spirit of the Living Water makes them bloom again. As I tilted my withered leaves towards the Son, I knew that with his loving favor shining down upon me I could once again flower.

> *A Tip for Foster Parents: When a person has hope, the Spirit of the Living Water makes them bloom again.*

God has a purpose for my life—and for your life. His purpose doesn't end leaving us broken and used up. He has wonderful things in store for us. He does not wish upon us evil but instead is ready to bless us with a future and a hope (Jeremiah 29:11). I went from depressed, devalued, and discouraged to renewed, remade, and reenergized. My mind and my body were healed!

As I returned home, I pondered the miracle of Jesus's birth that is celebrated during this Christmas season. I thought of Elizabeth, mother to John the Baptist and cousin to the Virgin Mary (Luke 1), barren and tired in her old age of waiting for the miracle of a child. Yet that was exactly when God chose her for the honor of bearing the anticipated prophet who would announce the coming of the Messiah, God's Son Jesus Christ (Luke 1:76).

God's timing is perfect. If I'd never had my tubes tied back in 2006, I would never have been willing to foster two precious children for three years. I may never know why God wanted me to say "yes" to them. But if God hadn't returned those same children back to their birth father, I would in turn never have been willing to take the necessary steps to once again carry a baby in my own womb.

From the Voice of Experience:

"My pregnancies were less than a year apart. The first time, I was filled with joy and expectations, the second time, dread. The first time I woke up my husband to tell him right away, knowing he would be overjoyed. The second time, I didn't even want to show him the test, knowing he would be passive. The first time, we told everybody, too excited to hold it in. The last time, we held our secret close as we waited for the worst. Having a miscarriage changed me completely. It was something I never imagined would happen to me.
When it did happen to me, I was so confused and lost. Why were my dreams taken from me before I had a chance to enjoy them? Working past the doubt and fear and sadness was one of the hardest things I've ever done. I wouldn't have managed without Christ. I had just asked Jesus to save me right before I lost my child. I had spent years running away from the Lord, trying to hide from him until finally he took my hand and told me to give in. And I did. I gave him all of me, and in return he gave himself for me.
Every time I woke up angry at the world for the loss of my child, he held me and promised me it would get better. When I feared I would never have another child, he told me that simply wasn't true. And as I tried to mourn the loss of my child, he told me to stop, for she wasn't gone but with him. Finding out I was pregnant again was hard, even though it was what I wanted. The Lord had done such an amazing work in me. I was no longer the same person. My life revolves around him and his path for me. I take my blessings when they come, but I also know I can sustain any hardship with

him by my side."
—T.R., a mom.

16 OUR MIRACLE

A new baby is like the beginning of all things: wonder, hope, a dream of possibilities. —Eda J. LeShan

I began the new year with renewed hope. One month went by, and I was not pregnant. The doctor had said it could take up to a year, so I resolved to be patient, trusting God to choose the right timing.

Then in February, our entire household was struck by a winter flu. We all took our turns being sick on the couch. Somehow in the process, I lost track of days. When I realized I might need to take a pregnancy test, I made myself wait a few more days, then braced myself for a negative result. After all, the flu could throw off a woman's internal clock. When the pregnancy test read positive, I had a hard time believing my eyes. Exactly forty-eight days after the surgery, I was pregnant!!!

Tim must have heard my scream as he came barging into the room. I'd wanted to plan a perfect way to tell him. But he had already peeked over my shoulder at the test results, exclaiming incredulously, "It worked? Already?"

The next day, a positive blood test confirmed that by October 2015 we would be the proud parents of another Lewis baby. Doctors take extra precautions with tubal reversal patients, since they experience ectopic pregnancies with greater frequency. A lot of tests confirmed my baby was healthy and growing normally. But around the sixth week of pregnancy, I felt pain and started bleeding. My heart sank. Would I never meet this miracle child, at least this side of heaven? Could I withstand another precious child being ripped from my life so quickly?

I prayed fiercely and constantly. At night, I would lie awake in bed for hours, praying. Sensing my turmoil, Tim would wake up and comfort me. He prayed over my womb and our unborn child. He also reminded me that lack of sleep and worrying only made problems worse. I had to relax. I had to sleep. I had to trust God again for healing.

I experienced intermittent bleeding throughout my entire first trimester of pregnancy. Each time, the process of worry would begin again. This included driving an hour and half to my doctor's office, listening for a heartbeat, crying tears of relief, then driving home again. It felt to me I was in both a spiritual and physical battle for the very life of this precious child.

After about my fourth scare, Tim pleaded with me to remain home: "Let what may happen be! Worrying and rushing to the hospital is not going to prevent anything. If anything, it is making matters worse."

My doctors all agreed with Tim that so long as I experienced no pain, I could stay home. Miraculously, once my baby entered the second trimester, all bleeding stopped. But the labels of "threatened miscarriage" and "advanced maternal age" kept me on my knees praying for this child. I prayed fervently for God to walk with me and allow me to know this child. While I didn't feel much movement compared to my other pregnancies, all tests showed the baby to be developing perfectly.

In fact, I could not have asked for a better pregnancy. I felt great. I soared through the second trimester and into the third, confident that everything would be smooth sailing from here on out. My doctors had recommended a Caesarian due to a previous C-section and my tubal reversal, so we scheduled the surgery for October 14, 2015.

September came, and I felt invincible. So much that I signed myself up to help Tim bring in the harvest. We have pigs, cows, and chickens that need fed and maintained. But my husband is primarily a grain farmer, and for the harvest he needed drivers. Even at eight months pregnant, driving isn't a hard job, consisting mainly of transporting grain from the field to the grain elevator. The hardest part for me was climbing up and down the steps of the massive tandem-trailer truck. But I took my time and it thrilled me to be participating with my husband in the harvest.

Since we heat our home with wood, we all work together in the fall chopping, sorting, and stacking our winter wood supply. I wasn't about to be left out, so I did the sitting jobs and never felt fatigued or an ounce of pain.

Another of our family traditions was volunteering with an organization called Food for Orphans that supplies nutritious meals to international orphans. Our purpose of volunteering was two-fold. One, we wanted our children, including our foster children when they were still with us, to give back into the lives of children more destitute than themselves. Two, we wanted to participate in missions as a family.

Since 2011, Tim and I had served as area coordinators for the organization, helping local churches raise money and organize FPEs, or Food Packing Events. In these events, participants prepare thousands of individual nutritious meals by repacking bulk supplies of rice, dried vegetables, soymeal, and other items into meal-sized packages. Even children can help, and the events are always filled with energy and excitement.

Our local church had scheduled a Food Packing Event on September 19, 2015, for fatherless children in Haiti. Since Tim and I were the coordinators, staying home was not an option. I didn't let my advanced pregnancy slow me down, walking countless steps, enthusiastically preparing meals, carrying many boxes of food, picking up trash, and of course talking to everyone. I loved to retell God's goodness in once again bringing a new baby to our family. By the end of the evening, I still did not feel even slightly exhausted.

September 20th dawned a beautiful fall day. After last night's frenetic activity, Tim insisted I take the day off from harvesting to rest up. I consented since my neighbor had invited me to bring our kids over to her granddaughter's birthday party. For Tim, it would be a long day in the fields, trying to get the grain in ahead of the forecasted rain, so I didn't expect him back until late in the evening.

My neighbor and I with other adults were playing Scrabble while the kids ran in and out of the house playing tag and other fun games. As I stood up to go for a drink, it felt as though my water might be breaking. I really wasn't sure, but I went home, leaving my children to continue playing. For the next couple hours, I rested and prayed. I couldn't tell if the leakage was continuing or I was imagining things. I called a friend and explained my symptoms. She insisted I call the hospital. So I did.

By now it was 6:30 p.m., and the last thing I wanted to do was drive ninety minutes to the hospital and ninety minutes back, not to mention wasting the time of the hospital staff, for what was probably a false alarm. Plus, I didn't want to pull my husband unnecessarily from the fields. But the nurse I spoke with kindly and insistently encouraged me to come on in. She'd already assigned me to a room, she informed me, so she expected me to show up.

Reluctantly, I texted Tim: "I think my water broke. Not sure. Going to head up to the hospital to be sure. Kids are at neighbors. Don't worry. Take your time and finish the field."

Then, I left for the hospital. As I drove, I prayed for God's protection over my unborn child and that God would give me a sign I had made the right choice in going. The last thing I wanted was to be a drama queen, making much ado about nothing.

The long drive to the hospital gave me the opportunity to begin a series of prayers. I prayed for the doctor who would be on call. If God was orchestrating something big tonight, such as the delivery of our miracle baby, I wanted God's choice of doctor to be on hand. I also knew the risks of delivering a preemie. I prayed God would prepare the baby for birth if it was this child's time to be welcomed here.

Looking back, I am sure glad God is in charge because that rushed journey to the hospital is not at all how I would have planned it. Since I was convinced it was a false alarm, I never even thought to bring the diaper bag we'd prepared or the infant car seat. I'd brought no change of clothing for myself, nor even a hair brush. I pictured myself getting to the hospital, then driving straight back after apologizing to the staff for being such a novice on birthing a baby. After all, my last had been over ten years ago!

By the end of the drive, I hadn't received the sign from God I'd prayed for. Getting out of my vehicle, I walked over to the ER door and pushed the ER call button. Just then, I felt a rushing surge of liquid. There was my sign. A full-fledged yes-your-water-really-has-broken sign!

Once checked into the room waiting for me, the nurses had me change into a hospital gown. I had gone to the restroom when I clearly heard the prompting of the Holy Spirit in my heart and mind: *Pray! Death is around the corner.*

My knees got weak, and tears rolled down my cheeks. A feeling of utter loneliness engulfed me, and I began to fear. I begged God to spare my unborn child. I pleaded for his mercy and for courage for whatever we were about to face.

Meanwhile back home, Tim had ignored my text to take his time and finish up in the field. Rushing home, he'd rounded up Caleb and Faith to help him feed the animals and pack bags for a trip to the hospital. Ten-year-old Caleb was helping Tim fill the stock tank with water for the cows when he suddenly looked up at his father. "Daddy, I have a bad feeling! Something is not right with Mommy."

Right there, Tim stopped what they were doing, and he

and Caleb prayed together. Truthfully, there is nothing better you can do. This feeling of urgency to pray is the Holy Spirit speaking to us, as he spoke to me in that hospital restroom. Prayer is not our natural tendency as human beings. The Holy Spirit leads us to pray, and he also intercedes for us before God's throne in words only God can understand:

> "Likewise the Spirit helps us in our weakness; for we do not know how to pray as we ought, but that very Spirit intercedes with sighs too deep for words. And God, who searches the heart, knows what is the mind of the Spirit, because the Spirit intercedes for the saints according to the will of God."
> (Romans 8:26-27, NRSV)

A Tip for Foster Parents: Prayer doesn't need to be fancy. The Holy Spirit can take our heart's utterances and present them holy before God.

In that moment, I had absolute certainty there was a battle for the life of my child. The devil cannot create life. Only God can. So Satan delights in destroying what only the Creator can give. That is why there is such a war when it comes to the unborn. A baby is a potential follower of God. This child could grow up and powerfully impact the kingdom of heaven, creating havoc in Satan's empire.

Piling our kids in his truck, Tim headed north towards a gas station where he'd arranged to meet his dad, who would take the kids to his home an hour away so Tim could drive on to the hospital. Tim hadn't driven far when a tire exploded. Caleb and Faith later told me it had sounded like a gun shot.

Turning the truck around, Tim had to drive it on the rim all the way back to our home and get another truck. By the time he made it to the gas station, handed the kids off to their grandfather, then drove to the hospital, it had taken twice as long as a normal drive to the hospital. A tire repair man who later fixed the tire said he'd never seen a tire explode in that particular fashion in forty years of tire repair. The battle was becoming fierce. Tim had to get to the hospital in time for our child's birth, and Satan clearly did not want that to happen.

Meanwhile, the hospital staff had warned me they would proceed without Tim if he did not arrive within the next half-hour. I wasn't quite thirty-six weeks along, so the baby would be about five pounds. I was given a choice to deliver again by C-Section or to try VBAC (Vaginal Birth After Cesarean). Since the natural process of delivering a baby is beautiful and a far easier recovery for the mother than a C-Section, I readily agreed on a VBAC.

But before the half-hour was up, Tim finally arrived at the hospital. When consulted, he insisted on a C-Section, asserting the risks were too great for a VBAC given my medical history and the prematurity of the baby. We would understand just why Tim's presence in the delivery room was so essential as that decision would save the life of our baby.

Just after midnight on September 21st, 2015, we entered the operating room for what Tim and I assumed would be a quick, straightforward operation. As the nurse administered spinal anesthesia, my body would not stop trembling, making it hard for her to insert the gigantic needle. I could not think of my own words to pray, so I began reciting out loud the only scripture that came to mind, Psalm 23, known as the Shepherd's psalm: *"The Lord is my shepherd, I shall not want . . ."*

I reached the part of the psalm that says, *"even though I walk through the valley of the shadow of death, I will fear no evil."* At that very moment, my body relaxed. I no longer trembled. I was not afraid. Death's ugly face did not scare me. The team of doctors and nurses surrounding me felt like a visible manifestation of God's power and protection. I praised God as they laid me down in preparation for surgery. The presiding doctor asked me if I was ready.

As the anesthetic took effect, I asked the doctor to pray for me. I can still hear her words ringing in my ears: "Lord, guide my hands."

I couldn't actually see the surgery since a curtain shielded the operating field from me and Tim, who sat beside me holding my hand. I knew time was crucial and that a C-Section shouldn't take very long. So as minutes ticked by, I grew anxious. When Tim jumped up to peer over the curtain, he was told to sit and stay sitting.

Then a nurse announced, "Eight minutes!"

I knew this was longer than a Caesarian should take. Something must be wrong. I started to cry. My body was being rocked back and forth. Blood was rapidly filling up disposal bags beside Tim. It seemed an eternity before a nurse announced, "It's a girl."

She immediately added, "Sorry, Daddy, you can't hold her."

There was still no cry of a newborn. Another eternity passed, though I found out later it was just three minutes. Then a weak cry broke the tension, and everyone in the operating room cheered. We learned that our baby had to be resuscitated with oxygen. Miraculously, only a few minutes later, our new daughter, whom we named Lydia Elizabeth, was in my arms. She was 4 pounds, 11 ounces, 17 ½ inches long, precious and perfect.

Only after the birth did Tim and I learn that if I'd gone into natural child birth, our new daughter possibly would not have survived, due to a condition called Vasa Previa. This occurs when fetal veins connecting the growing fetus within its amniotic sac to the placenta form outside the gelatinous protection of the umbilical cord, leaving them exposed and vulnerable to rupture. Too much activity such as I'd filled my days with in past weeks and the evening before, my water breaking, carrying my daughter the remaining weeks to term, the physical strain of natural labor—any of these could have ruptured one of those veins, leaving Lydia to bleed out within minutes.

Undetected, the infant mortality rate for Vasa Previa is 95%. Today, Vasa Previa may be discovered through a specialized prenatal ultrasound. But even with ultrasound, such as my own case, it is often not detectable before the baby is delivered, typically stillborn, and the placenta can be examined.

That Lydia's birth is an absolute miracle is undeniable. First, there was God's perfect intervention and provision of just the right skillful North Carolina doctor to perform a successful tubal reversal. Then for eight months, I was carrying a ticking time bomb around inside me, yet God protected me and my baby from rupture even with all the circumstances.

An even bigger miracle was how God sent me to the hospital at just the perfect time. Vasa Previa is incredibly rare, only one out of twenty-five-hundred births. When it can be properly diagnosed, the recommended procedure is a scheduled C-section at 35-36 weeks of pregnancy, the optimum balance between risks of rupture and risks of prematurity. That was precisely the time when God broke my water to send me to the hospital. He also inspired my husband to insist on a C-Section, which saved our daughter's life.

Even more amazing, the doctor who performed the surgery shared with me later that she had never so much as seen an image of a Vasa Previa. But just the evening before as the emergency surgeon on call, she'd been flipping through Facebook on her phone and had come across a Facebook posting about Vasa Previa. It had been on her mind as she dozed off, one reason she'd recognized the condition when she was called to carry out my emergency Caesarian.

Lydia and I stayed in the hospital for eight days. It was a grueling time, right in the middle of harvest. Tim would wake up early and drive to the hospital to have breakfast with us, then drive back and work until midnight. Every hour counted for Lydia with the fragility of her premature birth. I had lost an immense amount of blood, and my body did not have the hydration to produce the milk needed for the baby. As the Holy Spirit had spoken to me, Death was indeed just around the corner.

But God, who knew in advance I would have Vasa Previa and orchestrated the miracle of Lydia's safe birth, was the true head doctor for my pregnancy, and Death could not stand against his power and protection. While in the hospital, I listened non-stop to praise and worship music, a reminder of Who I had to thank for this miracle. Every chance I had, I removed Lydia from her incubator, placing her on my chest where we would listen together. I still remember the day she smiled to the lyrics of Kari Jobe's Forever:

> "Now death, where is your sting? Our
> resurrected King has rendered you defeated."

On the sixth day of my hospital stay, my milk supply finally came in. And on the eighth day, Lydia, at 4 pounds, 5 ounces, and I were both released to go home. The doctor had already explained to me one other consequence of Lydia's birth. Due to complications of the Vasa Previa and emergency caesarian, any attempt to carry another child could be life-threatening. I knew without any doubt that her explanation was God's word to me that he had not only fulfilled his promise and answered my prayers, but had completed his work for Tim and me in regards to having more birth children.

The story of Lydia, for whom our daughter was named, is told in the New Testament book of Acts (Acts 16:14-15; 40). She was a hard-working woman who heard the Word of the Lord and immediately put her faith into action. My husband chose this name for our daughter as a testament to Lydia's story. In the first century when she lived, women were devalued and Gentiles were despised by God's people, the Israelites. Lydia was both. Yet God chose her to receive the gospel of Jesus Christ, and she in turn used all she had to give back to God's people, sharing her faith with her entire household and offering the hospitality of her home to the apostle Paul and his companions.

We want our own Lydia's story to be a living witness to the power of following God. We want her very life to lead others to be active for the Lord. I am not ashamed to tell anyone who sees my child of the restoration my husband and I have experienced through her life. I will boldly tell people of this miracle that God has given to us.

Every time I gaze upon the lovely face of our precious youngest daughter, I am filled with awe at the way God has used our lives to tell his story. I do not yet understand all the whys of everything God allows to happen to us. But I have stopped asking that question. Instead of asking God why, we need to ask how. Not why is this happening to me, but how can I use this moment for God's glory?

> *A Tip for Foster Parents: Instead of asking God **why**, we should ask **how**. Not why did this happen, but how can I use this for God's glory?*

The difference takes our eyes off ourselves and places them on God. Once our eyes are on him, our God moves mountains. He separates waters so we can walk on dry land. He gives us fields filled with milk and honey. His promises are good and true. He will never forsake or abandon us, and he has good things in store for us. He is a good Father, and when we trust in him, we will see him do all things well. Like the prophet Isaiah exclaims:

> "Lord, you are my God; I will exalt you and praise your name, for in perfect faithfulness you have done wonderful things, things planned long ago." (Isaiah 25:1)

From the Voice of Experience:

"One thing that has really stood out to me in my life is the power of prayer and God's love for us in prompting us to pray. I once read that the strength or power that we have in comparison to God's is like a small battery compared to a power plant, and the power cord to connect us to his power is prayer. I love all the different ways he lets us know that he is near and available! It might come in the form of a young boy to whom he has given the gift of discernment saying, 'Daddy, I have a bad feeling. Something is not right with Mommy.'
When Caleb's daddy was in college, my routine chore of buying groceries was interrupted by a nudging to pray for him. I began to pray in the grocery store, only knowing that Tim was kayaking a river near Yellowstone at the time with his father and two younger siblings. What began as a gentle nudging to pray turned into a very strong urging to leave the store, go out to my car, and cry out to God for him. I soon found out why God sent such a strong and clear prompting to pray for Tim. His kayak had tipped over in a log jam on the river, and he had been pinned under one of the logs. The timing was exactly when God had me leaving the grocery store to pray. Praise God for his care for us and the privilege that he gives us in prayer to connect with him!"
—D.L, a grand-mom.

17 FULL CIRCLE

If I could relive my life, I would devote my entire ministry to reaching children for God!—Dwight Moody

As Christians, we too often have the mentality that we are somehow owed a happy, safe, trouble-free life where tragedy, pain, sorrow, failure, and disappointment should never be allowed to touch us. And if such things do touch us or others, it is someone's fault, possibly even God's doing. I don't think we do this consciously. I think most Christians have the best of intentions in wanting to lead a life that is completely victorious.

But what happens when bad things happen to good believers? Somewhere deep inside us, we too often believe the lie that God is punishing us. As in the Old Testament account of Job, Job's friends knew that God had to be punishing Job when he lost all his animals, his crops, and his ten children (Job 1-2, 4:7-9). If we are honest with ourselves, we often feel the same when we go through pain. We equate suffering with punishment.

When I started the journey of fostering, I knew that with God on my side, we would be victorious. After all, the apostle John assures us that the One [God] who is in us is greater than the one [Satan] who is in the world (1 John 4:4). I had no chance of losing. I would have a successful adoption story, and all who saw my family would witness God at work.

But when our foster children were returned to their birth parents, those who saw me instead shook their heads, commenting that our experience was precisely why they would never foster. More than once, I was told, "I could never give them back! That is why we will never foster."

This attitude angered me. Did our apparent failure to

provide a forever home for T-Man and Kay-Kay justify doing absolutely nothing to help such children? I had no real answer to respond to such comments. And I too was blaming myself at times for the loss of our foster children. Maybe I just wasn't good enough.

Having to return children to a home where they may not be appreciated and where their security is uncertain has been intensely painful. I am not naïve to the reality that they too might eventually fall into the trap of drug abuse like their birth parents. Or that they too might repeat the life style choices that would have their children end up in foster care. I know too well the many evils they may be exposed to on a daily basis in their new lives. My mistake was believing that these children were mine and that I was their "superhero" who could protect and provide for them. In so believing, I was usurping the place of God.

> *A Tip for Foster Parents: Children are ultimately God's children.* **He** *is their Provider and Protector.*

I have come to realize T-Man and Kay-Kay were never mine to begin with. And even when they were in my custody, I was incapable of providing the protection and provision that only Christ can guarantee. Even my birth children are not mine. Every child is God's child. God is the One who ultimately protects and provides. Can he protect my two precious former foster children even amidst evil influences and an ungodly environment? Of course, God can! To limit God's power based on whether or not I am in the picture is sinful.

What I've learned and need to remember every day is that everything I "own" is not really mine at all. Not even my body is my own. Everything I have is a temporary gift I will end up losing. Even my breath will eventually expire. I have no ownership in this life. So how is it possible to say I could lose something I never really owned? Jesus tells us in God's Word:

> "If you cling to your life, you will lose it; but if you give up your life for Me, you will find it." (Matthew 10:39, NLT)

When we give up our own life, we are surrendering the outcome to God. When I lost T-Man and Kay-Kay back to their birth dad, I believed I was defeated and that the devil had won because I could only see one positive outcome: adoption. But God has a way of seeing what we cannot see. He sees the whole picture. I am thankful I cannot see the whole picture or I might not have the courage to take on those tasks God has given to me. God has shown me that taking care of a child for even just one day is a blessing.

Today, my position on fostering has completely changed. It was a true gift to be able to have T-Man and Kay-Kay in our home for three years. It was also a gift that they returned home, taking with them the message of Jesus. As the church, the body of Christ, God's hands and feet on this earth, it is imperative we be willing to open up our homes for a day, a week, a month, or years to needy children in our communities. We should not view the system nor the birth parents as the enemy. We need to be willing to help birth parents meet their goals and receive back their children even if this results in pain or loss for our own hearts.

I was wrong to believe I was better than the birth parents. God has taught me that he loves the birth parents just as much as he loves their children. He has taught me to have compassion for the birth parents and to understand what a miracle it is for them to be reunited with their children. My heart tends to go down the path of self-righteousness again and again in regard to our foster children's birth parents and their failures. So I appreciate this quote from the well-known Christian author, theologian, and pastor David Jeremiah:

> "What a strange thing the heart of a believer is! It is often filled with righteous indignation against the sins of others while it is blind to its own. Just in proportion as a man is in love with his own sins and resentful of being rebuked, he will be unduly severe in condemning those of his neighbor."

It was a struggle for me to stop criticizing the birth parents and their many faults in parenting. After all, my own sins aren't any purer or holier. Yes, I have a great heart for justice and protecting the innocent. But too many times I viewed myself as deserving of our foster children and the birth parents as undeserving. Obviously, that kind of thinking does not come from our Creator. Those feelings of self-righteousness are evil.

I also believed that justice for our foster children required humiliation and loss for the birth parents. Thankfully, God doesn't work that way. God gives us all many, many chances. I may not be an addict or a felon according to our nation's laws, but I have needed forgiveness for my anger and my countless felonies against God's laws. Compassion puts others above ourselves. Compassion allows others to "win" even if it leaves us feeling that we have "lost". I was a temporary home for our foster children. And even if that wasn't our original intent in fostering them, it was an honorable, compassionate thing to do.

> *A Tip for Foster Parents: A 'temporary' foster home is just as valid as a 'forever' adoptive home. It is a compassionate, selfless act of love.*

Christ Centered Motivation

I pray that more Christian families will rise up and not be scared to be a temporary home for needy children within our communities. We don't need a signed adoption paper to love children. We don't need our last names behind children's first names to accept them. If I ever foster again or am given the opportunity to adopt, I will do it differently. My motivation will be different. Before and during our foster experience, I was motivated by hopes of adoption and providing a permanent home to the children. My motivation was truly self-centered. I believed I was the only mom these children could have if they were ever to be successful in life.

That misconception caused me to grieve immensely when our foster children left our home. My self-righteousness also generated great fear after they left. After all, if I wasn't there to be their mom, protecting and nurturing them, how could they possibly survive? My pride and confidence in my own abilities gave me a very limited perspective of who God is and how God works. Ultimately, God does not need me to keep these children safe. I am a tool in his hands, not the other way around.

These days I see things differently and I pray very differently. When it comes to fostering, I believe it is important to try to keep families intact. Even if a mom offered me her child for adoption, I would beg her to let me help her do whatever necessary to keep her together with her child. Maybe a family just needs someone to watch their kids for a few hours after school. Maybe a dad needs time to develop his own parenting skills through a supportive network. It may be more difficult to help a family stay together, and it will certainly be messier. But God has given those children to that parent, and that is not a mistake. We should be willing to help keep families together.

> ***A Tip for Foster Parents:** We should be willing to help keep families together, by providing loving support and encouragement to the birth parents.*

Not everyone is called into fostering. I understand that. But without a doubt, if you are a follower of Jesus Christ, you are called to help the widow and the orphaned (James 1:27). Help takes many different forms. We can all do a little something to help if we are brave enough to see beyond ourselves. I see "widows" every day; they are called single mothers. I see "orphans" every day too, children being raised with limited parental involvement. The opportunities to help are limitless.

Adoption does not have to be our only goal. I was so focused on the desire to adopt that I could not see any other goal. I could not picture myself as just a temporary mom. Yet if I am truly honest with myself, I am just that even to my birth kids. My home is not my birth kids' "forever home". Someday they will make a home of their own without me. For my foster kids, it just came a lot faster than I'd anticipated. But my desire to help the fatherless and abandoned should not end because I did not get to adopt.

Our lives are so short, and time is so precious. When I reach life's end and God calls me home to heaven, I want to make sure I have lived my life with no regrets. While we were still fostering, a friend who saw our children playing and laughing told me, "I've always wanted to adopt." When I chose to have the tubal reversal, someone else told me she'd wanted to do the same but couldn't find the strength. I never want to look back at my life and say, "I wish I would have . . ." However, little it may be, I want to do something today to fulfill whatever call the Holy Spirit has placed on my heart. I want to have big dreams for tomorrow.

I know the dream I had of adopting was a broken one.

The experience was a vital lesson for me to keep on learning. How well will I handle it when God takes away a dream? How should I respond when God says "no"? This doesn't just apply to adoption, but to every part of our daily lives. God can say "no" to anything, even good things like a business endeavor, getting married, having children, even a missions opportunity. How well do I trust when God takes something away from me that seems so righteous and good? Will I still trust him? Will I still continue to dream?

I think it is okay to grieve when God changes our dreams. God understands our tears (Psalms 56:8) and knows how to comfort us. He wants us to acknowledge our loss to him. He can then restore our failed dreams and give us new ones. Our joy must be found in him and not in the dreams itself. With God as the center of our dreams and desires, our hearts can repurpose themselves, and we can be open to doing things we never thought possible.

I still dream of the fatherless. My heart still yearns for the orphaned. I am in constant prayer for children who have no protection, no love, and no provision. At the same time, I also pray for the childless. The empty womb of the infertile. The foster parent who grieves every day for her foster child who remains emotionally unattached. And for the mother with a rebellious, runaway son or daughter who could be still alive or dead for all she knows.

There is much work to be done. I came across a quote, attributed to Adrianne Simeone, founder of The Mama Bear Effect, which seeks to protect children from sexual abuse, that expresses this well:

> "People ask, how can a person abuse a child? I ask, how can so many "good" people not do anything about it?"

Good question! We need more people with the courage to say, "That's it! I will make a difference. My home will at least be one home that offers a safe-haven for the broken."

Tim and I will always be advocating for the fatherless. Today, my goal is to be there for our own birth children and to help their friends who have single parents raising them. We want to open our home to these kids so they can witness a functional, God-fearing home. That is one small dream. But Tim and I have bigger dreams. We want to offer up the blessings God has given us, including our experience in fostering, to be mentors to fragile families within our community. We would like to help kids stay together with their parents.

This is a dream I would never have if we hadn't lost our foster kids back to their parents. I would still be thinking adoption was the only way to go. With this new dream, I have come full circle. As author and well-known women's Bible study teacher Beth Moore once said:

> "We know we're coming full circle with God when we stand at a very similar crossroad where we made such a mess of life before, but this time we take a different road."

For me, the "different road" is a new mentality. No longer do I believe that God punished me through the loss of our foster kids. God blessed me and changed me even through my grief. He not only loves the fatherless; he loves the faithful foster parent who is willing to risk it all for his sake. He wants good things for us. And he gives them to us freely. His will is, after all, beautiful. I can promise you that if you surrender to his will, your life will overflow with blessings. Yes, we will walk at times through pain. Scripture describes the follower of Jesus Christ as being crucified with him:

> "I have been crucified with Christ and I no longer live, but Christ lives in me. The life I now live in the body, I live by faith in the Son of

God, who loved me and gave himself for me."
(Galatians 2:20)

Part of being "crucified with Christ" means to embrace agony. A crucifixion is painful. But it also means that even when we suffer in this world, we will never be alone. Christ, who loves us and gave himself for us, lives in us. He gives us grace and will never leave us.

Pain does make us strong. In pain, we can grow and learn in ways we could never have done if life held no losses. I could never had imagined I would be where I stand today. But God planned it perfectly in advance. And even amidst great pain and perplexity, God has given me extraordinary joy. In this journey of loss, God was glorified.

> *A Tip for Foster Parents: Through pain we become stronger and grow in faith. God's eternal blessings will far outweigh any temporary pain.*

One day when Jesus and his disciples encountered a blind man, the disciples asked Jesus who had sinned for the man to be born with such a terrible disability. Was it the man himself or his parents? Jesus responded:

> "Neither this man nor his parents sinned. But this happened so that the work of God might be displayed in his life." (John 9:3)

Are you willing to be blind for God so God can use you when he wants to? Are you willing to trust that God can use your impaired vision and inadequacies to show light for a dark world to see? When to the world it appears you are a failure, will you dare to remain faithful to God, trusting he will lift you up in his perfect timing?

I hope you have answered "yes", because God is seeking

throughout the earth for those whose hearts belong completely to him (2 Chronicles 16:9). And his blessing that awaits you is more than you can ever imagine or plan. His everlasting blessing will far outweigh any temporary pain (2 Corinthians 4:17).

Guard Your Heart

In conclusion, I have been asked what advice I would give to those who want to help others by fostering or adopting. I did not understand until after our own journey of fostering was done, the truth of the statement that was originally given by a wise king thousands of years ago:

> "Above all else, guard your heart, for everything you do flows from it." (Proverbs 4:23)

> *A Tip for Foster Parents: Guard your heart. Reserve your heart for the Lord; make nothing else as important as your love for him.*

It's hard not to pour your entire heart into fostering. But that is dangerous, especially when the results of fostering are not as you had planned. As hard as it is, guard your heart. Make sure your heart is first and foremost reserved for God and that nothing else replaces your love for him.

Guard your heart when a social worker calls and says, "Dad wants a visit." Don't let your heart become discouraged.

Guard your heart when the court announces for the fifteenth time, "The goal is to return these children home." Stay on task to love those kids even though they do not have your last name.

Guard your heart when your child, whether birth, foster,

or adopted, grows up in your home, knows God's truth, yet decides to reject it. Don't believe the lies that all your hard work and tireless prayers were for nothing.

Guard your heart when you are suddenly alone, all your children swept away from you. You are not alone. God stands beside you. In his time, in his way, he will lift you up.

And above all, guard your heart by keeping it close to God's promises. For the heart is a fickle thing. It is naturally prone to wandering and distrust. Its desire is for the temporary things of this world. Without redirecting your heart, you will lose focus on what is true and find yourself slipping into despair.

We must, then, protect our hearts and teach our hearts to not be moved. If we love the Lord our God with all of our soul, all of our mind, all of our strength, and all of our heart (Mark 12:30), nothing else matters, win or lose.

As for me, my heart is content. My heart is in Christ Jesus. And I hold to the promise of God's Word:

> "May He give you the desire of your heart and make all your plans succeed." (Psalm 20:4)

From the Voice of Experience:

"As a social worker in Child Protective Services, I investigated over three hundred cases in three years ranging from minor to fatalities. In general, caseloads in child welfare are too high to be sufficiently managed. Overtime is common and often unpaid. On-call shifts are mandatory. Salaries are low and not reflective of the nature or intensity of the job. Policies and documentation requirements constantly change, and case managers are blamed for things entirely outside of their control. By the time I left CPS, I had been diagnosed with Post-Traumatic Stress Disorder as a result of the horrific events I had seen and heard. Child deaths due to abuse. Infant deaths due to neglect and Safe Sleep violations.

Children injured or killed by the misuse of guns. A five-year-old testing positive for cocaine. A toddler hospitalized in the burn unit. Deplorable and unsafe living conditions. A grade-schooler missing most of her teeth because her mom forced her to the floor and stomped on the back of her head. A girl requiring reconstructive surgery following a sexual assault by her mom's boyfriend.

One thing virtually all these cases have in common is that children are rarely in foster care or awaiting adoption due to any fault of their own. They are victims and survivors of things the adults in their lives have done to them or not done for them as well as the things that have been done or not done around them. In many instances, the cycle of abuse and neglect is generational with children caught in its web. There is a great need for families of all kinds to provide care for these children."
—A.S., a caseworker.

Will you respond to the need?

APPENDIX ONE:
A TRIBUTE TO THE CHILDREN WE LOST AND LOVE

You and I will meet again. When we're least expecting it. One day, in some far-off place, I will recognize your face. I won't say goodbye, my friend. For you and I will meet again . . . One day you belonged to me. Next day, I just wouldn't know. Someday, all the rules will bend. And you and I will meet again.—Tom Petty and the Heartbreakers

Now we see things imperfectly, like puzzling reflections in a mirror, but then we will see everything with perfect clarity. All that I know now is partial and incomplete, but then I will know everything completely, just as God now knows me completely.
—I Corinthians 13:12, NLT

Before T-Man and Kay-Kay left our home, I wrote a tribute for each of our foster children, which I gave them as a parting gift. Below is a partial abbreviation of those tributes.

To T-Man

Your story began before you ever came into our home. After I had received a call that you were coming, I began praying and God gave me a vision of you. I saw you walking down a church aisle. You were about nine years old. I could see the back of your body. You were bold. You were determined. You were radiant. I saw you accept Jesus as your Savior, and I saw you become adopted forever into his family. I saw you before you came.

T-Man, when you first came to us, you just amazed me. Our caseworker told me you had Cerebral Palsy, which you do have. It affects your right side of your body. You also had an IEP that classified you as developmentally delayed—eighteen months behind your peers. But did that stop you? No!!! We all worked hard after school hours.

The things you had to go through! Sometimes you would beg not to do physical therapy. It was hard work, and sometimes it hurt to stretch your muscles. I cried a lot for you. I wish I could have helped you sooner. I wish I could have known you earlier in life. But God knows best!

T-Man, God can use the bad choices other people make, choices that impact our own lives, to bless us. It's weird but true. You've had to work harder than other kids your age. But you do it. It has made you stronger than any kid I know. You were recently tested again for an IEP. And guess what? You are now a straight-A student and have no need for an IEP! Everyone around you can see God working in your life. You don't have a disability; you have a gift. Always choose to use your gift to show others who God is in your life.

T-Man, I love you! You are such a blessing to our family. As you leave our family and are joined again to the family that brought you into this world, you are a different boy than when you first came to us. You are radically stronger, cleverer, and ready! It pains me that I didn't have more time with you. I wish I could be there for all the many more wonderful things you will achieve in life. My prayers are with you.

But more importantly, the God who showed his favor on our lives by bringing you to us for a time is the same God who will be with you always. He was with you before you were born. He was with you when you almost died at the age of two. He was with you when you had to say goodbye to Grandma to come live with us. He was with you when you learned hard things you had to do to get better and healthier. He was with you when you said goodbye to us. He is with you now.

As you can see, I cannot make you learn things. I cannot force you to ride your bike. I cannot even teach you how to throw a ball. All these things you have achieved so far you did because you wanted to. We encouraged you. We prayed for you. But you did it. Look ahead now to the future. You determine your future. Life is bound to throw you a curve ball as it did in the beginning of your life. The devil will always prowl around trying to destroy you (1 Peter 5:8). Look to Jesus to carry you. Don't look at us. Don't look at your parents. Don't look to anyone. Look to Jesus. Look to Jesus.

May your heart always love him. Love him with ALL you have and ALL he gives you. Choose Jesus every day. He will continue to raise you up to succeed.

My blessings to you always, my precious son,

Your Mommy Bess

To Kay-Kay

So what to say? It's almost three years, and now you must go back to live with your birth daddy. It's hard to be happy even though I am sure it is quite an achievement for your daddy to be drug-free and fighting to get you back. That, actually, I am happy about. But that also means my time as your mommy is almost over. And that makes me sad, very sad. You see, I love you. I fell in love with you. So, let me tell you about you.

Sometime in February almost three years ago, I got a call about you. I actually didn't believe it. I thought it was a joke. Because I longed for you but didn't think my dream would come true. I wanted another child, especially another little girl, to hold and love and shower with gifts. So before you ever came into my house, I wanted you.

When you arrived, you let me unbuckle you out of the car seat and you held my hand until we were inside my house. By 5 o'clock that very day, you accepted us into your heart by calling us Mommy and Daddy. I remember how blessed I felt to be included in your heart. I also remember feeling sad. I was sad because I wasn't there for you before. Sad because I had missed your first three years of life. Sad not to know when you first crawled, walked, burped, and smiled. Sad because it was through a lot of hurt that you came to me. And for that, I hurt with you.

As I look back into my journals that I wrote during our three-year journey, I write how I would get mad and ask God lots of questions. Remember, you can ask God anything! He is a big God, and he can handle any question you ask him. You see, when you came to us, the caseworker told us we could adopt you. And I believed it. So, I thought you were mine since day one. Then your birth daddy called to see you while he was in drug rehab. I was upset and mad. I didn't understand why you had to see him. I didn't understand a lot of things. Remember, it is okay to be upset when you don't understand things because in life lots of things that happen are out of our control. I was mad because it hurt you to have to go back and forth to see him and remember bad moments you suffered. I was asking God why children have to suffer.

And this is what God spoke back to me:

> *"'What men intended for evil, I will use for good.' (Genesis 50:20)*

"I will use these two small children to lead your family, their parents, the social workers, teachers, doctors, the church, and community to my love. Trust me. I have not left you alone. All you need to do is love in obedience to me today. Do not worry about tomorrow. I am with them as I am with you."

Kay-Kay, the Lord has not been blind to your pain, your scars. He knows all that you have seen and heard and felt. He has been with you and will seek justice. The Lord cares even more about you than I do. And now three years later, I can say without a doubt, that he will use your birth daddy just like he used us to bring healing to you and build you up for a promising future. He is restoring your family and will continue to bless you and keep you. Jesus loves you. Please believe this: God loves you! Never doubt how much he loves you. Jesus loves Kay-Kay so much!

Kay-Kay, we had our rough days with you. Sometimes you were quite the challenge. You taught me about my own lack of patience. You butted heads with me. You sometimes probably hated me. Many times, I thought you disliked me for sure. And I want you to know that I messed up a lot with you. I am a sinful person. I tried hard but failed often. I wanted to love you, but I also wanted to prepare you for the long road ahead. Many times, I failed to just love you. We had many apologies. And many great cuddles. That's what love is—repentance and acceptance.

And now as you read this, you may remember good days and bad days with us. You may remember days of confusion when you didn't understand why you couldn't be with your birth mommy and daddy. And remember, I don't have all the answers, but I know Someone who does. Please ask Jesus all your questions and quietly wait for his answers and read his Word.

I will miss you. I will miss your smiles, your hugs, your messes (yes, even your dirty underwear and socks you love to hide under your bed!), and your toys everywhere! I will miss you doing your homework so fast and your awesome reading. I will miss you eating, no, consuming ice cream. I will miss styling your beautiful, long hair. I will miss your laughter. I will miss seeing you learn new things.

And then there are bigger things I will miss, like not being there when you lose your molars or when you learn what it is like to become a young woman. I will miss watching you learn how to drive or when you get your first boyfriend (which better not be until you're 20!!!). I will miss your wedding and when you have your first baby (aw, a little Kay-Kay!). But I will have all of eternity with you if you choose to make Jesus your Lord and King of your life. Please choose Jesus. Then our eternities will be sealed together forever.

Never forget I did adopt you. I adopted you in my heart. You will always be there. Always.

Love, Your Mommy Bess

APPENDIX TWO: PRAYERS FOR THOSE WHO FOSTER

Not one single prayer is wasted. In Psalm 56:8, King David, who at that time had been seized by his enemies, cries out to God,

> "You keep track of all my sorrows. You have collected all my tears in your bottle You have recorded each one in your book. (NLT)"

If God keeps track of each and every tear, he surely hears each and every request made unto him. Each petition is presented before the Father and has eternal life-changing results.

During my fostering and infertility journey, I prayed the following verses as prayers. I believe that scripture-praying is an effective way to come before the Father. I have categorized each verse according to topic and marked in bold core words for emphasis. May these verses draw you close to the Lord.

Anger

Psalm 4:4: "In your **anger** do not sin . . . search your heart and be silent."

Psalm 37:8: "Refrain from **anger** and turn from **wrath**; do not fret—it leads only to evil."

Fear

Psalm 34:4: "I sought the Lord, and he answered me; he **delivered me from all my fears**."

Psalm 56:3-4: "When I am afraid, **I put my trust in you**. In God, whose word I praise—in God I **trust** and **am not afraid**. What can mere mortals do to me?"

Isaiah 8:12-13: "**Do not fear what they fear**, and do not dread it. The Lord Almighty is the one you are to regard as holy, **he is the one you are to fear**, he is the one you are to dread."

Isaiah 43:5-6: "**Do not be afraid**, for I am with you; I will bring your **children** from the east and gather you from the west. I will say to the north, 'Give them up!' and to the south, 'Do not hold them back.'"

Worry

Psalm 55:22: "**Cast your cares** on the Lord and he will **sustain** you; he will never let the righteous be shaken."

Matthew 6:34: "Therefore **do not worry about tomorrow**, for tomorrow will worry about itself. Each day has enough trouble of its own."

Matthew 11:28: "Come to me, all you who are **weary** and **burdened**, and I will give you **rest**."

Philippians 4:6-7: "**Do not be anxious** about anything, but in every situation, by **prayer** and **petition**, with **thanksgiving**, present your requests to God. And the **peace** of God, which transcends all understanding, will **guard** your hearts and your minds in Christ Jesus."

Grief/Sorrow/Loss

Psalm 34:18: "The Lord is close to the **brokenhearted** and **saves** those who are **crushed in spirit**."

Psalm 51:17: "My sacrifice, O God, is a **broken spirit**; a broken and contrite heart you, God, will not despise."

Psalm 126:5: "Those who **sow with tears** will **reap with songs of joy**."

2 Corinthians 1:3-5: "Praise be to the God and Father of our Lord Jesus Christ, the Father of **compassion** and the **God of all comfort**, who **comforts us** in all our troubles, so that **we can comfort** those in any trouble with the comfort we ourselves receive from God. For just as we share abundantly in the sufferings of Christ, so also **our comfort abounds** through Christ."

Philippians 3:10-11: "I want to know Christ—yes, to know the power of his resurrection and **participation in his sufferings**, becoming like him in his death, and so, somehow, attaining to the **resurrection from the dead**."

Cry for Help

Psalm 18:29: "With your **help** I can advance against a troop; with my God I can scale a wall."

Psalm 109:26-27: "**Help** me, Lord my God; **save me** according to your unfailing love. Let them know that it is your hand, that you, Lord, have done it."

Zechariah 4:6: "'Not by might nor by power, but **by my Spirit**,' says the Lord Almighty."

Luke 10:19: "I have given you authority to trample on snakes and scorpions and to **overcome** all the power of the enemy; **nothing will harm you**."

Wisdom and Guidance

Psalm 143:10: "**Teach me** to do your will, for you are my God; may your good Spirit **lead me** on level ground."

Proverbs 11:30: "The fruit of the righteous is a tree of life, and the one who is **wise saves lives**."

James 3:13: "Who is **wise** and understanding among you? Let them **show it by their good life**, by **deeds** done in the **humility** that comes from **wisdom**."

Perseverance/Endurance for a Daunting Task and Long Journey

Philippians 4:13: "I can do **all** things through him who gives me **strength**."

Galatians 6:9: "Let us not become **weary** in doing good, for at the proper time we will **reap a harvest** if we do **not give up**."

2 Thessalonians 3:13: "N**ever tire** of doing what is good."

Peace

Psalm 4:8: "In **peace** I will lie down and **sleep**, for you alone, Lord, make me dwell in **safety**."

Isaiah 26:3: "You will keep in **perfect peace** those whose **minds** are **steadfast**, because they **trust** in you."

Isaiah 32:17: "The fruit of that **righteousness** will be **peace**; its effect will be **quietness** and **confidence forever**."

Jeremiah 33:6: "Nevertheless, I will bring **health** and **healing** to it; I will **heal** my people and will let them **enjoy** abundant **peace** and **security**."

Prayer for Foster Kids, the Fatherless, and Orphaned

Psalm 10:17-18: "You, Lord, hear the desire of the afflicted; you encourage them, and you listen to their cry, **defending the**

fatherless and the oppressed, so that mere earthly mortals will **never again** strike terror."

Psalm 72:12-14: "For he will **deliver** the needy who cry out, the afflicted who have no one to help. He will take pity on the **weak** and the needy and **save** the needy from death. He will **rescue** them from **oppression** and **violence**, for **precious** is their blood in his sight."

Psalm 82:3-4: "**Defend** the weak and the **fatherless**; uphold the cause of the poor and the oppressed. **Rescue** the weak and the needy; **deliver** them from the hand of the wicked."

Jeremiah 22:3: "This is what the Lord says: Do what is just and right. **Rescue** from the hand of the oppressor the one who has been robbed. Do no wrong or violence to the foreigner, the **fatherless** or the widow, and do not shed innocent blood in this place."

Prayers for Birth Parents

Isaiah 49:8-9: "I will keep you and will make you to be a covenant for the people . . . to **reassign** its desolate **inheritances**, to say to the **captives**, 'Come out,' and to those in **darkness**, 'Be free!'"

1 Peter 4:8: "Above all, **love** each other deeply, because **love covers over** a multitude of **sins**."

1 John 4:12: "No one has ever seen God; but if we **love one another**, God lives in us and his love is made complete in us."

Prayers for God's Protection on Visit Days

Psalm 84:11: "For the Lord God is a sun and **shield**; the Lord bestows favor and honor; no **good thing does He withhold** from those whose walk is blameless."

Psalm 91:11-12: "For he will command his **angels** concerning you to **guard** you in all your ways; they will **lift you up** in their hands, so that you will not strike your foot against a stone."

Proverbs 2:7-8: "He holds **success** in store for the upright, he is a **shield** to those whose walk is blameless, for he **guards** the course of the just and **protects** the way of his faithful ones."

Proverbs 14:26: "Whoever fears the Lord has a secure fortress, and for **their children it will be a refuge**."

Prayers for Handling the Court System

Psalm 112:7-8: "They will have **no fear of bad news**; their hearts are steadfast, **trusting** in the Lord. **Their hearts are secure**, they will have no fear; **in the end** they will look in **triumph** on their foes."

Proverbs 15:1: "A **gentle answer** turns away wrath, but a harsh word stirs up anger."

Isaiah 3:10: "Tell the righteous **it will be well** with them, for they will enjoy the fruit of their deeds."

Isaiah 33:22: "For the Lord is our **judge**, the Lord is our **lawgiver**, the Lord is our **king**; it is he who will save us."

Luke 18:7-8: "And will not God bring about **justice** for his chosen ones, who cry out to him day and night? Will he keep putting them off? I tell you, he will see that they get **justice**, and **quickly**."

Waiting in Hope for Adoption

Psalm 27:13-14: "I remain confident of this: I will see the goodness of the Lord in the land of the living. **Wait** for the Lord; **be strong** and **take heart** and **wait** for the Lord."

Psalm 37:7: "**Be still** before the Lord and **wait patiently** for him; do not fret when people succeed in their ways, when they carry out their wicked schemes."

Micah 7:7: "But as for me, I watch in **hope** for the Lord, I **wait** for God my Savior; my God **will hear** me."

Hebrews 10:23: "Let us **hold** unswervingly to the **hope** we profess, for he who promised is **faithful**."

For Barren Woman: Prayers to the Life-Giver

1 Samuel 1:11: "And she made a **vow**, saying, "Lord Almighty, if you will only look on your servant's misery and remember me, and not forget your servant **but give her a son**, then **I will give him** to the Lord for all the days of his life...""

Psalm 40:5: "Many, Lord my God, are the wonders you have done, **the things you planned for us**. None can compare with you; were I to speak and tell of your deeds, they would be too many to declare."

Psalm 113:9: "He settles the **childless woman** in her home as a **happy mother** of children. Praise the Lord."

Jeremiah 17:7-8: "But blessed is the one who trusts in the Lord, whose confidence is in him. They will be like a tree planted by the water that sends out its roots by the stream. It does not fear when heat comes; its leaves are always green. It has no worries in a year of drought and never fails to **bear fruit**."

Romans 4:19-21: "Without weakening in his faith, he faced the fact that his body was as good as dead—since he was about a hundred years old—and that **Sarah's womb was also dead**. Yet he did not waver through **unbelief** regarding the promise of God, but was strengthened in his faith and gave glory to God, being **fully persuaded** that God had power to do what he had promised."

Made in the USA
Monee, IL
22 January 2025

10490357R00115